TOUGH-MINDED MANAGEMENT

TOUGH-MINDED MANAGEMENT

A Guide for Managers Who Are Too Nice for Their Own Good

Gareth Gardiner

Fawcett Columbine • New York

A Fawcett Columbine Book
Published by Ballantine Books
Copyright © 1990 by the Smith Collins Company

This edition published by arrangement with the Smith Collins Company.

Library of Congress Catalog Card Number: 92-90376

ISBN: 0-449-90771-6

Cover design by Sheryl Kagen
Cartoons: Glen Klinkhart

Manufactured in the United States of America
First Ballantine Books Trade Edition: March 1993
10 9 8 7 6 5 4 3 2 1

TO MAUREEN, MY WIFE

TO FRANCES AND JAMES,
MY PARENTS AND MY CHILDREN

TABLE OF CONTENTS

INTRODUCTION

The Power and the Pain of Tough-Minded Management

Are you just too nice for your own good? Are you tired of feeling helpless while you watch problems get worse? Are you fed up with having your employees manage you? These types of questions appeared on the back cover of the first edition of this book, and they appear again on the back of this edition. They appear again because they have touched a nerve ending in the psychology of contemporary management: We have an over-abundance of modern managers, both men and women, who are just too nice, and who inadvertently make employee problems worse because they are afraid of the conflict that might result if they take action to deal with problems of the two-legged variety.

Ah, the temptation and the pain of avoidance. Avoiding a problem situation may buy us a little time, during which we can kid ourselves (''The problem's temporary, it'll soon go away''), but the end result will almost always be that the problem will get worse, and be even more painful to deal with than if we had taken prompt action and resolved it before it became a crisis. Since the first edition of this book appeared, dozens of managers have come forward at seminars and business meetings to testify to the enduring truth of the proposition that managerial avoidance normally makes matters worse, and may even create hell on earth for the manager who is truly chickenshit.

This latter expression has more than touched a nerve ending: It has provoked merriment, intense interest, and even disgust among the truly nice; however, it has never produced disagreement with the very serious managerial proposition embodied within it. Gutless avoidance of employee problems, and of management problems in general, is a prescription for disaster.

Those of us who strive to avoid pain, or who fear conflict, simply create more of it in our lives, particularly in the long run.

The power of the notion of tough-minded coping with problem employees is precisely that most of these problems can be solved if they are dealt with promptly, even though conflict may result and relationships may be strained in the short run. The manager who solves problems rather than makes them worse is a precious commodity everywhere in a world of excessive niceness, and this little book represents a modest but practical attempt to help managers become a bit more tough minded and a lot more successful in handling the messy, mind-boggling, and wonderful problems that employees can present.

How This Book Is Organized

Yes, there is a logic in the way this book is organized. Chapters 1 and 2 discuss the rise of the nice guy in management, along with why excessive niceness is the Achilles heel of any manager. Humorous examples highlight both the perils (and the virtues) of being nice. Chapter 3 develops a model of managerial effectiveness, which shows that tough-minded management is a sensible middle-of-the-road alternative to both nice-guy and tough-guy managerial extremes.

Chapters 4 through 8 lead us through a basic five-step tough-minded model for coping with virtually every category of problem person. Chapter 4 discusses how and why to set up effective interviews with employees; Chapter 5 shows the manager how to state problems effectively and get results by simply doing that; techniques for clarifying problems and learning not to prejudge employees are examined in Chapter 6. Chapter 7 is doubly important because it shows the manager how to close interviews effectively—by getting promises of action from employees that will resolve problems, as well as how to refer employees for professional help, or to fire them gently but firmly when there is no alternative. Chapter 8 ties up the loose ends and discusses the importance of documentation and following up problem-solving interviews.

Chapter 9 takes on the world. The tough-minded problem-solving model laid out in the previous five chapters is generalized to deal with real-world problems, such as the taking of Americans as hostages, problems of drug abuse in the workplace, and the eternal problem of unpaid bills and how to deal with creditors. All the chapters have numerous short examples of tough-minded management in action, with lots of tips for dealing with specific problems, like a carpenter who drinks too much or an employee who smells too much. Some of the examples are not particularly nice, but that is what this book is all about: Reading it may help you become a better manager, or at the very least, help you understand employee situations better.

ACKNOWLEDGMENTS

The talented persons who have helped in the preparation and publication of this book are all owed a hearty vote of thanks. O. C. Ferrell has been as fine a partner as an author could hope for. Gwyneth Vaughn's editing has been sensitive, loving, and highly professional. Curt Neitzke has been both competent and creative in designing and producing the book, while Glen Klinkhart has drawn the delightful cartoons that illustrate it.

Cathy Boehlke, Ruth Mullenix, and Linda Prante have been most helpful in typing and retyping the manuscript at various stages of development. Lastly, my wife, Maureen, has been loving and supportive and patient at times when the author's fitful temperament would have tried the patience of a saint.

Chapter 1

THE RISE OF THE NICE-GUY MANAGER

*I think that managements in this country are sadly
lacking—not all managements, I want to make it clear—there
are some very good managements. But generally speaking, I
think we have a great crisis managerially. What has developed
is a sort of anti-Darwinian pattern where you have the survival of the unfittest. Just like college, where the president of
the fraternity is a real likable guy, the president or the CEO of
the company is usually a likable guy. In college, you remember, the president of the fraternity was always around to go
drinking with, and he was your friend, and he was fun to have
at parties. But he wasn't the guy that you would have picked
to run your family business.*

*The same thing has developed over the last twenty years
in management.*

—Carl Icahn[1]

"Nice guys finish last," observed the baseball manager Leo
Durocher many years ago. Ironically, this pithy aphorism has
become even more relevant for contemporary Americans and
American management. There is increasing, and indeed overwhelming, evidence that everywhere in America we are suffering from an overdose of the "nice-guy" syndrome: Nice guys
run major corporations, manage the military, and hold high public offices. Young people report in survey after survey that one of
their major goals in growing up is to be nice. Niceness has
clearly become an important theme in American life.

At first blush, it is difficult to disagree with the principle
virtues of niceness: Nice people are socially pleasant; they keep
their bodies clean and odor-free; they go out of their way to be
considerate of others; and they are ever so likable. When you're

ill, they send you cards and letters; when you're broke, they make you a quick loan; and they will agree with your opinion on just about any topic. The expression, "He's a nice guy," has all sorts of positive connotations. Nice people are thoroughly and completely agreeable; they don't make waves; and they are found in abundance at social gatherings everywhere.

As is the case with almost any virtue, however, niceness can rapidly become a vice when carried to extremes. Niceness becomes a problem when it leads to the almost-compulsive avoidance of conflict and to paralysis of decision making. When it becomes more important to be agreeable and to be liked than to deal with a difficult and disagreeable problem situation, niceness leads to ineffective and self-defeating management. That is precisely what happens when nice guys become milquetoast managers and begin avoiding problems.

The Achilles heel of the nice person is the need to be liked, carried to extremes, accompanied by a strong fear of being disliked. Of course, in the management of other people, this fear has disastrous consequences. For example, when a manager allows an employee to come in late day after day, pretending that he or she doesn't even see the employee arriving and taking no action whatsoever to change the tardy behavior, a sea of trouble is bound to ensue. Not only will the tardy person's behavior begin to deteriorate, other employees will begin to take advantage of a manager they rightly judge as gutless, and who, in even plainer terms, they contemptuously refer to as "chickenshit."

What is most sad about such a situation is that the manager's intense need to be liked leads to exactly the opposite result. He becomes an object of amusement and contempt, loses the respect of the entire group or organization, and ultimately loses his job because of the poor performance and low morale of the organization. Months or even years of inaction create a situation in which effective management and discipline become progressively more difficult, and an atmosphere of cynicism and hopelessness becomes pervasive.

Why Nice Guys Become Managers*

If one may somewhat oversimplify the history of American management, it is (firstly) boring, and (secondly) a chronology of a breaking away from authoritarian, uncaring, and exploitative management techniques. In the 1950s and 1960s, distinguished scholars and management theorists and scholars such as Douglas McGregor,[2] Abraham Maslow,[3] and Rensis Likert[4] wrote eloquently and insightfully about the sins of traditional American management. They argued in both learned journals and the popular press that coercive and punitive management practices are inherently self-defeating and that in the long run, they produce deeply alienated and unproductive employees.

Their point was well taken, and while one could choose from literally thousands of supporting examples, perhaps one of the more dramatically illustrative is the history of management/labor relations at the Ford Motor Company. The hiring of vicious goons by that firm in the 1930s to prevent, often violently, attempts by the United Auto Workers to organize the firm's workers, coupled with the company's extreme slowness to adapt to changing standards in compensation and working conditions, led to long-term labor problems for Ford. This is not to single out Ford in this regard, because such authoritarian techniques were the norm in American industry, and they led directly to the rise of strong labor unions in such key industries as steel and auto manufacturing. The early history of the American labor movement was primarily the drive to establish some basic human rights for workers.

By the 1970s, the combination of scholarly input and worker-initiated changes led to a growing recognition and acceptance of the shortcomings and weaknesses of traditional management, where the worker was at best a cog in the organizational wheel. Maslow, McGregor, and their colleagues found attentive audiences throughout the land, and their disciples and converts not only continued to spread the word but also began to develop training and selection programs based on more humanistic principles. The thrust of these programs, irrespective of their content, was good and decent. Supervisors and managers were encouraged to become more considerate toward employees, to involve them in

---

*It should be noted at this point that throughout this short volume, the term "nice guy" is used generically, and is not specific to either sex. Men certainly have no monopoly on nice-guy management. In general, there is probably even more pressure placed on women, unfortunately, to be "nice." The term "nice person" has not been used because it has so little sex appeal.

decision making, to listen more effectively to their problems, and in general, to treat them better.

One of the unanticipated outcomes of this new emphasis on humanistic management, however, was that it became one of the factors contributing to the rise of the nice guy in management. Maslow and McGregor would have rolled in their graves had they known that their earnest and laudable preachments would, in many cases, become justification for the selection and promotion of likable individuals to responsible supervisory and leadership positions, individuals whose pleasant and considerate behavior was also marked by a strong reluctance to deal with problem situations and by a fear of unpleasantness and conflict: a pattern of behavior the Gestalt therapist Fritz Perls accurately called "chickenshit avoidance."[5]

There is no question that American organizations, both public and private, have come to be dominated by nice guys, and that this phenomenon has developed roughly over the past twenty-five years. As Carl Icahn noted at the beginning of this chapter, likable people may be fun to be around and to have a drink with, but they do not necessarily make the most effective leaders. While it might make a fascinating academic exercise to identify all the historical factors in American society that have led to the ascendance of the nice guy, for the purposes of this volume it is probably more useful simply to note a few societal influences and then get on to what to do about it.

How Americans Became Nice People*

The historical American was decidedly not a nice person. For openers, the conditions of pioneer life pretty much precluded the development of any significant number of nice or wimpish behaviors on the part of early Americans. When life was a busy and frequently dreary routine of scrambling to raise food, hustling to build adequate shelter against a formidable cli-

---

*Since the author is widely regarded in his circle as a nice guy and has many days when chickenshit behavior is dominant in his behavioral repertoire, he would like at this point to apologize to the American Historical Society and all serious students of American history for this fast and loose treatment of the phenomenon of niceness in our country.

mate, and fighting to save one's life from the attacks of savage Indians (who had not yet been civilized by the great white father and turned into nice persons), the behaviors that were valuable were somewhat rude. The rural pioneer American had to be self-reliant, physically aggressive, blunt and tactless, and entrepreneurial just to survive.

Since conformity processes sometimes tend to be treated as an unmitigated evil by contemporary social scientists,[6] it might be useful to take a quick look at why a fairly high degree of conforming behavior is necessary to survival in an urbanized country in which people live in close physical proximity to each other. People who conform are predictable, understandable, and nonthreatening. This is particularly true when one of the key values in a conforming culture is being pleasant or nice to other people. If you can depend on other persons in your immediate urban environment to be nice, you can move around relatively freely without having to be constantly vigilant to ward off physical danger. While this value may have gone slightly amok in contemporary urban America, the causes of the problem are so complex that they demand treatment elsewhere.*

The other development in American society that was to a large extent caused by industrialization was the development of large organizations for the accomplishment of work. Corporations became large because this was a good way to maximize output and profitability. Government organizations then became large in an attempt to control the excesses of the first large corporations, which were family owned and run by a class of not-nice people who uncharitably came to be referred to as "robber barons." People like the Rockefellers, Morgans, and Carnegies, who were not only profit motivated but who were also brilliant organizers and entrepreneurs, thrived in an unregulated business environment.

As corporations continued to grow throughout the twentieth century, and as more and more became publicly owned, bureaucratic, as opposed to entrepreneurial, values tended to become more dominant throughout industry. Government agencies and organizations were already thoroughly controlled by bureau-

---

*The perceptive reader will already have detected that the author shamelessly resorts to avoidance whenever it suits his purposes.

crats, of course, and the convergence of these values between the private and public sectors became another reason why the nice guy ascended to a position of prominence in American management.

Why the Cream Does Not Rise to the Top

Individualistic, outspoken, creative, entrepreneurial persons by and large do not succeed in rising to the top, or even to managerial positions, in contemporary large American organizations—nice guys do. Entrepreneurs are a particularly difficult commodity for the bureaucratized organization to handle. They simply do not play by the rules; they are abrasive and outspoken; they are often contemptuous of the ideas of others; and they normally want to run their own show.

As the psychologists Jacob Getzels and Paul Jackson noted some twenty-five years ago in their studies of creative schoolchildren, the creative child has a very difficult time in an institutional environment,[7] for roughly the same reasons as the entrepreneur (who in most cases is well above the norm in creativity). Creative schoolchildren are frequently disliked by their teachers; entrepreneurs are hated by bureaucrats.

In the large organization, the nice guy gets ahead because he or she is socially pleasant and agreeable. The nice guy follows directions and takes orders well and doesn't make waves. He is attentive to organizational politics and tends to align himself on many sides of many issues. The nice guy avoids confrontations, and he is a complement to almost any social occasion. He works hard enough and well enough at his job that he rises up the organization. The Peter Principle—which most simply stated means that persons are promoted until they reach their level of incompetence,[8] at which point they are dead-ended—is at work.

When the entire organization becomes top-heavy with nice guys, however, organizational disaster can unexpectedly occur. Not only does the company lose creativity and become vulnerable to the innovations of aggressive, frequently smaller competitors, the entire company can suddenly be snatched from the hands of the nice guys who run it by the predatory onslaughts of a not-nice T. Boone Pickens or Carl Icahn. These avant-garde entrepreneurs of the late 1980s are well aware that when nice guys are faced with conflict and threat, they panic.

The corporate raiders have come to have a certain élan. They are almost folk heroes, and this is probably due less to any good they are supposedly doing (it is the nice guys, after all, who do good work) than to the fact that they have stampeded entrenched corporate management. One of the less agreeable characteristics of the nice guy, when he has made it in the organization, is that he builds a nice nest for himself. In large corporations, this means creature comforts such as corporate jets, country club memberships, and large offices. It somehow strikes the average person as only just when an executive earning more than $1 million a year in salary and bonuses, but who is losing money for his company, gets his comeuppance from a raider.

The Seamy Side of Being Nice

Since the nice person wants to be liked and desperately wants to avoid conflict, sometimes some fairly tacky strategies have to be used to maintain the appropriate image. The avoidance strategy that is most often used, but not often discussed because it isn't nice, is lying. A *U.S. News & World Report*-CNN survey found that 60 percent of a national sample believe that their spouses sometimes lie to them.[9] A few years ago, a St. Louis radio station conducted an informal poll of its listeners, which revealed its typical listener told upwards of thirty lies a day. While the poll was completely unscientific, many people hearing the results of the survey simply shook their heads in disbelief. The results are nonetheless true.

While many of the lies we tell are designed to make us look more important ("I was the head of the whole operation."), and while fishermen are not to be judged in normal terms, most lies are told to avoid conflict and to make us appear nice. The classic social lie, "I'm sorry I can't make your party because I'm going to be out of town that night," is a good example. We often compound this lie by adding, "but I'd really love to be there!" The real reason we can't make the party, of course, is that we don't want to because we consider the hostess a complete twit and her

7

guests tiresome nerds. We don't want to say this because such judgmental behavior would put us in a bad light and do serious damage to our image of niceness, and because it would seriously offend the hostess. The lie thus becomes a "white lie" and is judged to be harmless.

While much social lying is undoubtedly harmless and necessary to keep human relationships tolerably pleasant, the pervasiveness of lying in our society is more worrisome. We have evidence, for example, that the American consumer does not believe the claims of virtually all advertisements, and that American voters do not believe the statements of virtually all politicians. According to the *U.S. News & World Report*-CNN poll, politicians have significantly lower credibility in the eyes of the average American than auto mechanics.

While the author will not make portentous or profound statements on the phenomenon beyond those already offered, in recent years he has begun leading discussions on lying in graduate business classes. These sessions are invariably fascinating and wonderfully refreshing, and follow a somewhat predictable pattern: (1) There is initial embarrassment about the fact that there is so much social lying and lying on the job; (2) there is much laughter and virtual catharsis in the class as different lies are discussed; and (3) pledges are made to reduce the amount of lying to facilitate relationships, make sales, or reduce conflict. Some student reports to the class after such pledges have been made are delightful and demonstrate that we do not always have to use avoidance to reduce conflict. One (anonymous) student, a manager in the marketing department of a food-processing firm, made the following report:

> I've always hated going to the damned weekly department meeting, so I'd usually skip it, and lie to my boss that I couldn't make it because I was sick or busy or something. I'm sure he never believed me, but I never told him the truth—that I thought the meeting was a complete waste of time and that if we met once every two or three months, we'd accomplish a lot more. So anyway, after we talked about lying in class last week, my boss asked me if I was going to the meeting tomorrow, and I thought about what we'd discussed in class, and I said, "No, I'm not because we could get more done if we met like every three months." Well, at first he looked like he might

have a fit, and I thought I'd better clear out my desk because I might be fired, but then he looks at me and asks why I think so, and since it's too late to go back now anyhow, I tell him again, and we talk about it for ten minutes or so, and he says, "You know I agree with you, Joe, but I've always kind of felt we had to hold the meeting because we've always done it." He thanked me for being honest, went back to his office, and sent out a memo saying we'd meet once every three months except if most of us felt we really needed a meeting. Everyone's happier now, and we get more done.[10]

Aside from the courage demonstrated by the student in taking the risk of being honest with his boss, perhaps the most beautiful thing about this encounter is that it broke the back of the psychology of fear. Not only did the feared outcome, termination, *not* take place, a constructive change occurred that led to greater harmony and productivity. At this point, it will be cheerfully concluded that honesty is the best policy, and that the worst lies we tell are those we tell ourselves.

A CONSTRUCTIVE DIALOGUE

Let's stop for a minute and look at the nice-guy syndrome in practice. The following dialogue illustrates a first-line management dilemma with a reasonable solution.

"You Ain't Their Buddy No More"

Martin Greensleeves has been a foreman at Lawrenceville Steel, Inc., for five years and is currently supervising a group of twelve men. Most of the men in his group had been coworkers prior to his promotion, and Martin had experienced some expressions of anger and jealousy from men who had long been his friends before he became foreman. Thanks to good management and a lot of patience and understanding on his part, these conflicts were ironed out.

Martin was not greatly surprised when Tom Chaney, who had been promoted to foreman only a few weeks before, approached him one day at work and asked if they could meet. As the two men sat in a quiet corner of a nearby tavern sipping beer, Martin asked Tom why he had asked for the meeting:

Tom: Martin, I wanted to talk to you because I've really been worried that my men don't like me no more, now that I'm foreman. Some of them have been kind of cold to me.

Martin: Well, Tom, didn't you kind of expect that when you got promoted? You know, when I made foreman, they wouldn't talk to me for a while, and they started making wise-cracks about my getting too big for my britches, and how stuck-up I was. I just kinda laughed and tried to be friendly, and I figured it'd blow over.

Tom: Yeah, that's kinda what's been happening to me. It sort of hurts that guys like Big Joe, who used to joke around with me all the time, are acting a little snooty. I mean, I been buddies with these guys for years. We all been fishing together for years, watched ballgames on the tube together, and just been good friends.

Martin: I can see it's hurting you a bit, Tom, but just keep acting normal and friendly, and they'll start to come around.

Tom: Well, yeah, that's kinda what I've been doing, and I'm glad that Big Joe came over this afternoon and asked if I'd go out for a beer with them Friday night, just like we've been doing for years, but that's what I wanted to ask you about, Martin, do you think I should do that? Because I wanted to be friendly, I told Joe, sure, I'd join 'em, but do you think I did the right thing, I mean we've been buddies forever?

Martin: Well now, Tom, sure I think it's great you're going out for a beer with them, but there's something you've got to remember—you ain't their buddy no more, you're the boss—and that means some things gotta change.

Tom: What do you mean, Martin?

Martin: Tom, when you're the boss, you're the boss, and you can't change that. That don't mean you can't be

	friendly with them, and you gotta act like a real jerk, but you just can't be their buddy no more. Do you know what I mean? I had to make some changes when my old pals asked me out right after I made foreman.
Tom:	What did you do when they asked?
Martin:	Well, I just said sure, I'd join them for a beer, and I did. Friday night we went to Smokey Joe's just like always, and I made sure I ordered a couple of pitchers of beer. I sat there and I shot the breeze with them for a while, and I finished my beer. Then I got up and I said, "Hey, I really enjoyed the beer, guys, and I hope you have a great weekend, but I gotta run. I'll see you all Monday." I waved goodby, shook a few hands, and then I split. Know why I'm always the first to leave, Tom?
Tom:	Yeah, I think I can guess. It has to do with you being the boss, right?
Martin:	You got it, Tom. If I sit there all night sucking on a beer, and I get glassy-eyed, falling-down drunk with them, what the hell am I gonna say to 'em on Monday morning when they stagger in late with a big head. When you're the boss, you gotta be the boss, Tom, but you can still be an O.K. kinda guy, but you gotta realize things have changed.
Tom:	Yeah, I see what you mean, Martin. I sure appreciate the tip.

On Friday night, Tom Chaney joined his long-time friends at Smokey Joe's tavern for a beer. After finishing his first glass of beer, he got to his feet, wished his employees a happy weekend and said goodbye. His friends shook his hand, wished him well, and continued drinking beer after his departure.

ENDNOTES

1. "The Man of Steel," *Newsweek,* October 20, 1986, p. 52.

2. Douglas McGregor, *The Human Side of Enterprise* (New York: McGraw-Hill, 1960).

3. Abraham H. Maslow, *Motivation and Personality* (New York: Harper and Row, 1954).

Abraham H. Maslow, *Eupsychian Management: A Journal* (Homewood, IL: Richard D. Irwin, 1965).

4. Rensis Likert, *New Patterns of Management* (New York: Random House, 1961).

5. Frederick Perls, *Ego, Hunger, and Aggression* (New York: Random House, 1969).

6. David Reisman, et al., *The Lonely Crowd* (New York: Yale University Press, 1950).

7. Jacob Getzels and Paul Jackson, *Creativity and Intelligence: Explorations with Gifted Students* (New York: Wiley, 1962).

8. Laurence J. Peter and Raymond Hull, *The Peter Principle* (New York: Morrow, 1969).

9. *U.S. News & World Report*—CNN poll by the Roper Organization with Everett Ladd of the Roper Center for Public Opinion Research, *U.S. News & World Report,* February 23, 1987, p. 57.

10. Statement made by a Lindenwood College M.B.A. student, 1985. Available from the author as a videocassette.

A CASE OF NICE-GUY
MANAGEMENT RUN AMOK

The Lecherous Lecturer

Dr. Harvey Hornytoad was a professor of sociology at a major Midwestern university in the 1970s. He was a handsome, silver-haired man, and he spoke with an urbane and sophisticated Oxford accent. However, his courteous and pleasant professional manner belied the nature of his nocturnal classroom activities. In his dealings with students, and with women in general, Dr. Hornytoad was a legendary and relentless lecher. The "lecherous lecturer" soon became his sobriquet.

In his sexual deviance class, which met in the evening, Dr. Hornytoad was known to lecture in the nude, standing proudly in front of an astounded class. He openly and blatantly propositioned female students: "If you want to earn an "A" in this class, my dear," he would purr, "You must have sex with me." His most outrageous departure from accepted standards of professional behavior, however, was the fact that he was known to have sex with students in his office. Although the door to the office would be closed, moans and groans could be heard from within at not infrequent intervals.

The university community was scandalized, of course. Husbands of female students wrote angry letters to the president of the university, Dr. Walter Wimpish, and professors and other members of the community inundated him with furious phone calls. Wimpish, whose academic background was in philosophy, was at his wits' end as to what to do. Nothing in his academic training, nor in his career as an academic administrator, had prepared him for this type of situation.

After many consultations with his advisers, and after much soul searching, Wimpish decided that the appropriate course of action was to offer Dr. Hornytoad a positive letter of reference if

13

Nice-Guy Lesson #1

How to spot a nice guy...

Nice guys are always
being stepped on!

he would resign his position in the sociology department at the end of the current academic year. Hornytoad gratefully accepted this offer, and was shortly hired by another university some two-hundred miles away. During his tenure at that institution, he also committed numerous sexual indiscretions, although his behavior was not quite as blatant as it had previously been. He was no longer known to have sex with students in his office, for example, although he continued to proposition female students.

After eventually being fired by the second institution on sexual harassment charges, Hornytoad disappeared from public view for several years. He resurfaced when he was arrested for molesting a six-year old girl in a large Midwestern city. He is currently serving a long prison sentence for sexual deviance in a federal penitentiary.

Chapter 2

THE CAUSES AND CONSEQUENCES OF MANAGERIAL AVOIDANCE

A Veterans Administration supervisor in a Midwestern state noticed that his secretary was frequently very late to work on Mondays, and often did not come in at all. While he felt that this was wrong, he took no disciplinary action because he assumed the problem was temporary and that her attendance would soon improve. Within a few months she had completely stopped appearing for work Mondays, and began missing Fridays as well. Still, he took no action. After two years of letting her work three-day weeks while getting paid for five, he finally worked up enough nerve to call her into his office to advise her that she would have to begin coming in every day of the week, or she would begin losing pay. Upon hearing this, she flew into a rage and stormed out of his office yelling, "They don't treat people right around this damned place." He cowered behind his desk until she was safely out of sight.[1]

Why Avoidance Makes Problems Worse

One of the fondest beliefs of nearly every nice-guy manager is that if he's just pleasant to his employees, most problem situations will simply take care of themselves. As is the case with any rationalization, there is a grain of truth to this notion. Employees have just as many nice-guy tendencies as managers, and they too want to be liked. In general, when people feel that they are cared for and that they matter in an organization, they perform better. Unfortunately, when a nice-guy manager neglects to take effective action to deal with a problem and begins avoiding even the most casual daily contact with a problem employee,* that is not the message the employee gets.

For example, when a tardy employee arriving late to work for the third time this week sees his supervisor sitting behind her desk pretending not to notice, there are several messages that he might get from this behavior, all of which have potentially disastrous consequences for the manager. The first message is that the supervisor (and the company) simply doesn't give a damn. "Nobody cares for me around here. See, she's sitting behind her desk reading a newspaper. She couldn't care less that my car broke down again this morning, and that I don't have enough dough to get it fixed. She doesn't even care enough to ask me what's wrong. Why should I bother to put out any effort here?"

Since caring and trust are two of the psychological pillars of any effective society, the employee who feels neglected is also going to feel hurt and resentful. The most common and easy expression of these feelings in the workplace, of course, is to lie down on the job. The alert supervisor, who also has some understanding of the common causes of unproductive behavior, on noticing a period of pouting and resentful behavior from an otherwise cheerful employee, might take the opportunity to stop by that person's desk or work station just to chat for a minute or two. While there are probably no real one-minute miracles in management, a few minutes spent by the manager in chatting with an employee will often elicit a lot of spontaneously offered information.

A second message an employee might get from management avoidance behavior is that there are no performance standards in the organization: Anything is O.K. Come in late, come in drunk, it doesn't matter. This message can rapidly take any company down the road to ruin, and it is another of the unintended and unspoken but real messages underlying management by avoidance.

A third message received from managerial avoidance may be the most devastating. This is the perception that the manager has no guts and will never take action to deal with problems. The

---

*In this volume, a problem employee is very simply defined as any person who is not getting the job done satisfactorily, irrespective of the underlying causes of the unsatisfactory performances.

immediate consequence of this message is loss of respect for management, firstly by the problem employee who is getting away with unsatisfactory behavior, and secondly by the other employees in the work group or department. Because most employees are not stupid, a problem employee who sees that he or she is not going to be disciplined for missing work, as was the case with the secretary in the introduction to this chapter, is likely to take ever-increasing advantage of the situation.

There are at least two reasons for this, the first of which is that most nonwork activities are distinctly preferable to work, given the boring nature of the average American's job. When an office clerk, for example, realizes that his nice-guy boss is going to pay him when he knocks off for an afternoon to go to the old fishing hole, he's going to spend more and more time fishing. The second reason is that most of us, even those who are reasonably healthy adults, have enough childish and historical resentment and fear of management in us to take advantage of managers who will not use the legitimate authority they have. This game is made doubly exciting by the fact that it is charged with anger. It is always possible that old Chickenshit Charley might just get off the pot and give me (deserved) hell for the stuff I've been pulling! In the meantime, I'm just going to push him a little bit more every day, to see how much he'll take.

When other employees who are normally prompt and productive see a problem employee "getting away with murder," they go through a series of predictable reactions. The first of these is usually the hope that management will step in and do something effective to change the problem employee's behavior. The average person has enough pride in himself or herself, and enough motivation to do the job well, that he or she reacts badly to problem behavior. "Hey, this guy is not doing his job," or "This gal isn't pulling her fair share of the load," are two typical responses of other employees when a problem situation emerges. "Now I just hope old Charley does something about it," rapidly follows.

Famous last, sad words. After months or even years of watching Charley hide behind his desk, doing nothing while the problem employee's behavior continues to worsen, they too become problem employees. It is a basic proposition in fairness and equity: "Why should I bust my butt when this guy is getting away with doing nothin'? I'm going to go home at noon, too."

Management by chickenshit avoidance has at this point produced chaos, and the manager has descended into a personal hell on earth. He struggles with himself each morning to go to work. When he gets there, he can hardly bear to look at his malingering, complaining, do-nothing employees. He begins taking aspirins in bunches and has three-martini lunches. His own job performance deteriorates while he broods over the mess he has created. He contemplates taking action against this sea of troubles, but his own chronic avoidance leaves him paralyzed. He has done nothing for so long that it becomes progressively more difficult for him to do anything.

This is perhaps the most bitter outcome of chickenshit management—watching your office go to hell in a handbasket and feeling absolutely powerless to do anything about it. Rather like the strong fear of water that the near-drowning victim experiences; if she doesn't dive back into the water soon, her fear leaves her terrified of water for the rest of her life. The manager faces a powerful and complex emotional dilemma. He is filled with self-contempt because he knows that he has created the misery he lives in. For most of us, however, it is an easier choice to direct our anger outward, and at this point, the hapless manager finds himself filled with rage toward the employee whom he blames for the present predicament.

Finally, after months or years of avoidance, he snaps. Perhaps it is an unusually flagrant breach of the rules that does it, or perhaps it is just the long accumulation of aggravations. In any event, in a voice shaking with rage, he calls the employee into his office, slams the door and screams, "You're fired, you worthless piece of garbage!* You're through! I don't have to put up with any of your guff anymore! Now get out of here! Clean your desk and get out of here! I don't want to see your face around here again! Get out! Get out! Get out!"

A self-defeating tragedy now unfolds. The employee, who has been lulled into a false sense of security by long-term managerial inaction, flies off the handle at the abrupt nature of his dismissal. He does exactly what a nice-guy manager fears most and hurls epithets, barbs, and even the office furniture at the

---

*In anticipation of having large numbers of nice readers, the author has sanitized the colorful dialogue that often occurs during unexpected firings.

unhappy manager. The ugliest of confrontations ensues, often leading to physical violence, and the employee finally leaves screaming indignantly, "You wait and see, I'm going to sue you! I'll be back! You wait and see!"

The sad thing, of course, is that the employee *will* be back, with back pay, after a successful lawsuit. Because his case was not documented, because an orderly series of disciplinary procedures was not followed, and because assistance to help him cope with his problem was not offered, he has been handed a strong legal case. The company affected has now been handed an unhappy choice—spend thousands of dollars defending itself against a suit that it will probably lose, or reward the employee with a generous out-of-court settlement. Not surprisingly, many companies opt for further avoidance and spare themselves public embarrassment by choosing the latter.

A classic no-win situation has been created, as is the case with any neurotic behavioral pattern. The problem employee loses, even if he wins the lawsuit, because he goes back to work for a company for which he has worlds of contempt and that doesn't want him back. The supervisor loses because he may have to face the nightmare again, and in living color. The company loses because it not only has to pay high legal or settlement costs, but it also has to rehire an unproductive employee whose bad habits have been reinforced by years of managerial avoidance.

Because the long-term costs of chickenshit management are so high for everyone concerned, logical questions begin to be asked. Why didn't someone do something earlier? Why do problem-employee situations go unchecked and worsen year after year? Why is there so much managerial avoidance in America today? Unfortunately, there is no easy, logical answer to such questions. The answer, or at least part of the answer, lies in an understanding of the psychological roots of avoidance, and why such behavior is so widespread in our culture.

The Roots and Manifestations of Chickenshit Avoidance

Avoidance behavior, like any neurotically self-defeating behavior, is motivated by fear. Many of the fears that underlie neurotic conflict date back to childhood, when a person is more easily overwhelmed by its intense nature and significantly less able to cope with it in a healthy way. Many childhood fears persist into adulthood and drive the individual to engage in behaviors that promise to avoid or block the fear, but inevitably draw the person back to the fear and force him or her to re-experience it.

Because this analysis of the psychological roots of avoidance is somewhat abstract, it might be more helpful to identify some of the specific fears that underlie most managerial avoidance. In our culture, there are two fears that are common among persons raised to be nice people. One is the fear of being disliked or rejected, and the other is the fear that one has done a bad thing or is a bad person. This latter fear is usually called guilt. Nice-guy managers who are filled with guilt and are terrified of rejection unwittingly end up feeling bad most of the time and are disliked by their employees. Again, it is precisely efforts to avoid these fears that ultimately causes people to bring about the very things they fear.

As adults, when we experience rejection or commit a misdeed or make a mistake, we don't like the experience, but we also don't fall to pieces. It's usually not the end of the world. Although the pain of losing a loved one is very real, we know that the pain will eventually ease and that we will live happily again, that we will risk caring for someone again, and that we will take risks that might lead to major mistakes again.

The nice person who is filled with neurotic fear is simply paralyzed by it. The part of him or her that is a healthy and mature adult recognizes that he should take action, and take it now, to cope with the poor performance of an employee; but the lingering childhood fear is so strong that it produces complete inaction. The rationalizations and denials that follow the failure to act are almost laughable.

"The problem is temporary and will go away"—the classic cop-out. The problem will usually get worse. "I don't have any right to interfere in her personal life." When the employee is not getting the job done, the manager has every right—indeed, has an *obligation*—to intervene, whatever the cause of the problem. "I'm not a psychiatrist or psychologist, and it's obvious this person has a serious mental, drug, or alcohol problem. I could really harm him if I do something wrong." Naturally, the supervisor is not expected to be a mental-health professional, but it is inaction that will harm the employee most. Any person in the grip of a chemical dependency that he or she can no longer control will almost always continue to deteriorate when the problem is ignored.

As problems continue to worsen, a managerial form of avoidance is frequently attempted. It's called giving the problem to someone else. The most familiar form of this maneuver is the phony performance appraisal followed by the transfer to Peoria. To get rid of the problem employee, the manager first arranges to give the person a highly favorable performance rating, filled with glowing compliments and with all expletives, of course, deleted. The employee is then abruptly transferred, often with no prior warning, to another department or agency.

This mechanism is self-defeating, not surprisingly. The employee moves to his new environment with all his problems intact. The old bromide that "a change will do him good" is usually just wishful thinking. The new supervisor, who anticipates that she has inherited a veritable superstar, soon discovers the nature of the scam that has been visited upon her and reacts with predictable anger. The nice-guy manager, while relieved to be rid of the problem at last, continues to wallow in feelings of low self-esteem because at bottom, he knows full well that he has copped out again.

A variation of the transfer ploy is to send the employee off to the personnel department for disciplinary action. "Well they've got professionals there who can deal with this," is one line that often accompanies the move. Another is, "Well they gave him to me in the first place, so it's their responsibility anyway." This strategy may have more to recommend it than the transfer, because someone in the personnel department may in fact take action on the case, but it is still a cop-out. The personnel department will normally be ill-equipped to handle a problem-employee situation, because its professional priorities are elsewhere. Also, when the product of someone else's chronic avoidance is suddenly dropped into personnel's lap, it is unreasonable to expect effective action on a crisis basis.

Why Guilt Is So Common and Why We Need to Be Liked

Since feelings of guilt and the fear of being disliked are such powerful dynamics in avoidance and nice-guy behavior, it is well worth spending a moment or two to understand why they are so prevalent in our culture. Guilt has its roots in all the messages we get in our society from parents, educators, and (sometimes) the church, that we are "bad." As parents, we can rapidly produce neurotic feelings of guilt in our children when they drop things, for example, by saying, "You're a stupid, clumsy, bad kid!" Most children weep when they hear such parental statements, because no child wants to be bad.

The use of such guilt messages to control behavior has powerful consequences, the worst of which is that many of us as reasonably healthy adults have lingering suspicions about our real worth. This phenomenon is most clearly seen when highly successful professional people feel deep anxiety about their success, attribute it to luck, and fear that they will soon be discovered as the phonies and frauds that they believe themselves to be, and that their success will be temporary. Recent studies have shown that anywhere from one-third to one-half of all successful adults have such feelings.

Feeling guilty about success is doubly sad because the individual not only lives with the fear that he or she will be "found out," but also loses sight of the real reasons for his success, which usually have to do with intelligence and hard work. Guilt and the fear of being disliked are interrelated, and an implicit message in being disliked for many persons is that they are bad. Only good people are popular and successful, the belief goes. To be liked is to be good, and to be liked, one must be nice. Being nice means being unrelentingly pleasant and agreeable, and not losing one's temper.

What the outcome of all this is, plainly, is a lifetime of fear and appeasement (and chickenshit behavior). The ghosts of the legendary Caspar Milquetoast and the more contemporary Dr. Walter Wimpish are alive and well in America.

What Nice People Do or Don't

Feelings of guilt and the need to be liked underlie many

rather humorous behaviors that nice people engage in (or are forbidden to engage in, as is more usually the case). The major "do" for a nice person is to be unfailingly pleasant and self-effacing. The nice person does not put his or her needs or desires ahead of others. This is often a prescription to be rolled over and stomped upon because it leads to behaviors that threaten psychological welfare and sometimes survival.

The following list of behaviors that are required of the nice person is by no means exhaustive.

1. Nice people do not eat the last food on the plate. It's always enjoyable dining in the homes of nice people because you know you're going to get the last piece of fried chicken or the last dinner roll. Sometimes really nice people will foil you in this regard, however, by putting out additional food.

2. Nice people do not brag about themselves. Nice persons have a tough time on job interviews because one of the 20 questions an interviewer will almost always ask is, "Why should I hire you?" The nice person is never prepared to say something good about himself, so he loses the job to someone who is.

3. Nice people do not laugh at sick jokes. So-called "sick" humor has the psychological function of helping people bear grief that might otherwise be unendurable, although some of the jokes are genuinely and deeply tasteless. Nice people do not *laugh*, however, at the notion that Karen Carpenter is the patron saint of Ethiopia, or that NASA stands for "need another seven astronauts."

4. Nice people do not make waves. Nice people can be counted on not to complain, and even to offer a tip when they are short-changed or get absolutely lousy service in a restaurant. Nice people are great to have at meetings because a determined zealot can get them to go along with almost any crazed scheme he or she proposes.

5. Nice people always praise new clothing, hair styles, or decor. No matter how badly the hair stylist has butchered your last cut or how tacky your latest discount dress looks, nice people can be counted upon

to reassure you that you look great: "Frankly, my dear, you look maahvellous!"

Avoidance, Avoidance, and More Avoidance

Although Fritz Perls once observed that avoidance never gains anyone anything,[2] avoidance is practiced everywhere, and American society certainly has no monopoly on it. The Japanese, while they are brilliant managers in other respects, go to great lengths to avoid dealing with problem employees. Their avoidance pattern, however, takes a uniquely Oriental form, and what is most distinctly Japanese is that both workers and managers normally participate.

Since the work group and its stability is highly valued throughout Japanese society, the group becomes responsible for rallying around the problem individual. This is usually accomplished by other members of the group compensating for the unproductive member's lack of performance during working hours, so that overall productivity will not be harmed. This is also where the intervention usually stops, unfortunately.

Because formally disciplining, counseling, or firing the unproductive employee would involve a mortal loss of face for that person, management will continue to ignore the existence of the problem for years on end, while the work group will continue to cover for the individual for an equal length of time. While one may admire the patience of the Japanese in this regard, the consequences of Oriental avoidance for the performance and problems of the affected individual are about the same as American avoidance.

Alas, every form of human avoidance is known to every chickenshit manager everywhere. Procrastination is universal. Denial is done in dozens of nations. Lying makes the world go round, and lately even the Russians seem to be demonstrating nice-guy tendencies. Cynics would say there is no escaping a world of niceness, but in this volume there will be hearty disagreement with that hypothesis.

A CONSTRUCTIVE DIALOGUE

Let's stop for a minute and look at nice-guy behavior and the role of guilt. The following dialogue illustrates that feelings of guilt can prevent a person from taking a necessary action or make a person miserable after making a very tough decision.

"Lisa"

Lisa Fowler decided to return to college to complete her degree in business. Although she had been a good student at an Oregon college and generally earned excellent grades, the strain of an impending divorce from her estranged husband had led to her decision to drop out of school temporarily the year before.

During a discussion in a managerial psychology class, the role of guilt feelings in human behavior came up, and she expressed keen interest in the topic. After hearing the instructor assert that guilt feelings generally leave the individual afraid to act and feeling bad about himself, she began to talk about the failure of her marriage:

Lisa: Well, that was certainly true of me. I had so many feelings of guilt that I hung in there in a real bad relationship when I should have left long before I did. Sometimes I feel stupid that I didn't leave sooner, but it was feelings of guilt and thinking I was a bad person that caused me to delay as long as I did.

Instructor: Can you tell us more about the relationship, and why it was bad for you?

Lisa: I sure can. I was married for two years to a man I cared for a lot, and still do. But during the time we were married, he only worked for a total of four months. It's not that he couldn't get jobs, God knows, he must have had six different jobs, but he wouldn't keep one for more than a few weeks, then he'd get bored and quit. He's such a smart guy, and personable. He'd get hired right away, every time he interviewed, but then he'd quit the job saying it wasn't right for him.

Instructor: You say he had a number of different jobs?

Lisa: Yes, he worked as a reservation clerk at the Holiday Inn, then as a waiter at a restaurant downtown, and then a worker in the City of Salem Parks Department. Then he got on with the company I work for, and he was excited about that for a while—said it was keeping us together—but he quit that one too, after about a month. I was so embarrassed because I'd helped him get the job. He'd always go a month or two after he left one job before he'd even start looking for another one. I finally got tired of the excuses and him lying around the apartment and never doing any of the house-work, but it was the time he didn't cook dinner that finally did it for me.

Instructor: What happened in that incident?

Lisa: He'd just quit the job with my company and had been staying at the apartment sleeping and watching television, and I came home one night after working all day and feeling real tired. Also, I had a class to go to that night at the college. Anyway, when I got home I could see he hadn't been doing anything all day be-cause the house was a mess, and there were beer cans all over, and the TV set was blaring, and then he said, "What's for dinner, honey?" Well, I just lost it, and I started screaming at him and told him to get the hell out because I was fed up with his crap. So he left and moved back in with his mother, and then I started feel-ing really guilty for throwing him out, espe-cially when he kept calling, saying how he missed me and loved me, and how bad he felt

	about quitting the job. He asked if he got an-other job, could he move back in and like a fool, I said yes.
Instructor:	You said, "Like a fool"?
Lisa:	Yeah, the biggest fool you've ever seen because he got another job alright, this time with the telephone company, and moved back in. The job lasted two weeks, and we were right back to square one with me working days and going to school nights and him lying around the apartment all day.
Instructor:	Sounds like it was pretty frustrating for you.
Lisa:	It sure was, but not for long. Even though I still felt like a heel and like I wasn't a nice person at all, this time I told him to get out and stay out. And I've stuck to that. For the first few weeks, I felt pretty bad because he called me every day, but when I went through with the divorce, he didn't even show up in court, and then he stopped calling me. I haven't heard from him now in over eight months. I still sometimes worry about him and wonder if I did the right thing. Do you think I did the right thing?
Instructor:	I certainly don't think you did anything bad, Lisa. Do you think you harmed him by getting the divorce?
Lisa:	Well, not really. He's a grown-up person, and I know he's got to make his own living, but I still worry and feel guilty. I know we've been talking a lot in this class how irrational most guilt is and that's sure helped me feel better, but I still worry about him at times. I don't want to get back together, please understand, but I'd just like to be sure I did the right thing.
Instructor:	Is there any way you can check that out without hurting yourself?
Lisa:	You know, I think there is.

Two weeks later, Lisa came up to the instructor after a class session, with a small smile on her face:

Lisa:	Well, I called one of my former husband's friends and asked what he was doing, not because I wanted to get back together, but just to see what he's doing and if he's alright. Do you know what his friend told me?
Instructor:	No, I don't. What did he say?
Lisa:	Well, his friend laughed and said that my ex-husband is working in a mill in southern Oregon, and he's kept the job for nine months. And he said that my leaving him was the best thing that ever happened to him because he knows now that he's got to grow up and make something of himself.
Instructor:	I'm happy to hear that he's working and sorry that he misses you. I hope you still don't feel you did a bad thing.
Lisa:	I sure feel better about what I did even though it still hurts at times, and I wish things had turned out better for us.

ENDNOTES

1. Developed and adapted from the author's consulting experience.

2. Frederick Perls, *Ego, Hunger, and Aggression* (New York: Random House, 1969): 17.

A CASE OF NICE-GUY
MANAGEMENT RUN AMOK

Mr. Rarely Redditt

Rarely Redditt was a tall, sensitive man who had been in the textbook publishing business for some 20 years; for the last three he had been a senior editor for West Coast Collegiate Publishers, a major publisher in the college market. West Coast had hired him out of a much smaller house in Wisconsin, where his work had been superb. He was recommended to West Coast's management as an extremely conscientious, almost meticulous editor, who gave scrupulous attention to even the smallest problems in a newly submitted manuscript.

When he joined the West Coast staff, he was given an office on the fifth floor of the office building where the company was housed. While he reported for work right on time at 8:00 A.M. for the first two months he was on the job, he immediately began to complain about the "open landscaping" concept employed by West Coast, which involved partitioning various work areas with moveable screens that did not quite reach the ceiling of the office area. He stated repeatedly that the open concept did not adequately muffle sound, and the noise level in his area was unacceptably high. "I just can't concentrate," he frequently complained, "with this damned racket going on all the time."

As his work load increased, so did the level of his complaining. When he was told by the president of the company that there was no immediate prospect that the open landscaping concept would be modified in the near future, he told his fellow editors that he needed time to go to the library or to the park to think, since he could not concentrate adequately on his assigned manuscripts in his office.

For the first two months after this practice began, he would disappear from his office one or two times a week, typically for

31

Nice-Guy Lesson #2

Nice guys will avoid confrontation.

an hour or two, and then he would reappear to finish the work day. His absences gradually increased until after his first eighteen months on the job, he was roughly splitting his time between the park or the library, and his office. After his second year he announced to his fellow staffers that because of the unacceptably high noise level in the office, he would no longer come in during normal office hours, but would make appearances evenings and weekends to pick up his messages and read mail. Otherwise, he said, he would work in the privacy of his home, with his telephone unplugged, so he could not be reached during the day.

No company official ever told him that this behavior was unacceptable. Occasionally the company president would attempt to shoot him a disapproving look, but this tactic was largely ineffectual because Mr. Redditt was so rarely in. Redditt's productivity dropped sharply during this third year, and the number of manuscripts that he edited dropped to less than half the number edited by any other editor at his level. At the end of the editor's third year, the president drove to Redditt's home, where he found him lying on a sofa watching television, and informed Redditt that he had been terminated.

Redditt angrily told the president that this was the first time anyone had told him that he was not doing a good job. He also said that it was obvious that West Coast Publishing didn't give a damn about its employees, because no one had ever made any attempt to change the office system so that the sound level would be less distracting.

Chapter 3

A MODEL OF MANAGERIAL EFFECTIVENESS

Albert Speer, who was Minister of Economics in Hitler's Third Reich, admits in his memoirs that he made a major mistake in employing slave laborers in some of the Nazi manufacturing plants. In one plant, where the laborers were making bombs, the workers were absolutely ingenious at sabotaging the weapons, even though armed guards were literally standing over them. They were also very adept at "playing dumb," constantly asking for instructions, and refusing to make the simplest decisions. Unless the workers were watched constantly, and even when they were, they would successfully misalign a bomb's fuse, and it would become a dud. Since the only practical way of detecting whether or not a fuse was functional was to drop the bomb on the floor, the Nazis resorted to hiring more and more guards in an effort to prevent the sabotage. At one point, the plant had nearly as many guards as workers.[1]

The Use and Abuse of Managerial Authority

The way in which a manager uses the authority available to him or her is a critical factor in determining managerial effectiveness. The nice guy, in his milquetoast fashion, shrinks from using authority and suffers all of the negative consequences of avoidance behavior. At the other extreme of the managerial authority continuum, however, is the *tough-guy* manager (see Figure 1). Even in a society increasingly influenced by middle-class values of niceness, this type of manager is still around.

Researcher Rensis Likert has shown that in the short run, authoritarian or tough-guy managers do get results, and this type

Figure 1 -- The Continuum of Managerial Authority and Effectiveness

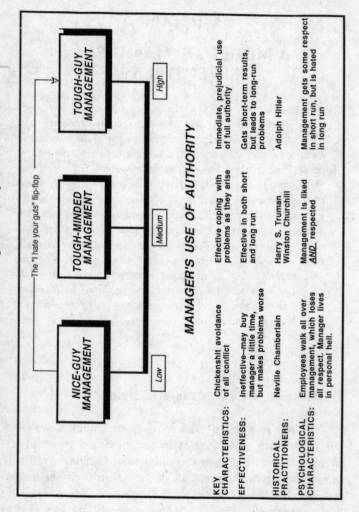

The "I hate your guts" flip-flop

| NICE-GUY MANAGEMENT | TOUGH-MINDED MANAGEMENT | TOUGH-GUY MANAGEMENT |

Low　　　　　　　　Medium　　　　　　　　High

MANAGER'S USE OF AUTHORITY

	NICE-GUY MANAGEMENT	TOUGH-MINDED MANAGEMENT	TOUGH-GUY MANAGEMENT
KEY CHARACTERISTICS:	Chickenshit avoidance of all conflict	Effective coping with problems as they arise	Immediate, prejudicial use of full authority
EFFECTIVENESS:	Ineffective--may buy manager a little time, but makes problems worse	Effective in both short and long run	Gets short-term results, but leads to long-run problems
HISTORICAL PRACTITIONERS:	Neville Chamberlain	Harry S. Truman Winston Churchill	Adolph Hitler
PSYCHOLOGICAL CHARACTERISTICS:	Employees walk all over management, which loses all respect. Manager lives in personal hell.	Management is liked AND respected	Management gets some respect in short run, but is hated in long run

of manager may have a spectacular organizational career if he is wise enough to keep hopping from one company to another.[2] This is the sort of person who is hired by a firm to come in and clean house. Typically, he inherits a deeply troubled department or work group, often left behind by a nice guy, and he promptly proceeds to lop off heads. His first move is often the abrupt firing of an employee chosen almost at random. A wave of fear sweeps through the organization and performance improves dramatically, in the short run.

In the long run, however, productivity begins to slump rapidly when there is a continuation of management by terror; if the tough-guy manager is so unwise as to linger too long in any one setting, he too finds himself on the way out. Over time, the power of fear to motivate improved performance diminishes: Fear simply loses its effectiveness. While a great deal of formal academic research supports this statement, perhaps the easiest way to prove the point is simply to talk to any child who has endured years of empty parental threats. "Don't you dare do that, Johnny, or Mommy will spank you." The child soon becomes remarkably and permanently deaf.

Another reason that tough-guy management simply doesn't work in the long run is that employees begin voting with their feet. Rather than endure continued abuse, employees who have relatively immediate job options begin leaving. Others become highly motivated to develop such options. The tough guy may lop off the deadwood in the short run, but in the long run, it is the most competent employees who leave, never to return.

A third reason for a long-term drop in performance is that employees who are forced to remain are never so ingenious and creative as when they are subverting management they hate. The short case that introduced this chapter illustrates the point beautifully. The familiar management cliche, "Don't get mad, get even," must have originated in an authoritarian organization run by exploitative, tough-guy managers.

In view of the fact that there is so much evidence that tough-guy management is ineffective over the long haul, another of these logical questions cries out to be asked: Why are there still so many authoritarian American managers around? The answer to this one probably lies in our perennial quest for a quick fix, for a miracle worker who can remedy our ailments overnight. The tremendous emphasis that we place on improving bottom-line performance quickly places American managers under tremendous pressure to produce now, often to the long-term detriment of the organization. If the Japanese have a single critical lesson to teach us, it is probably that we need to be more patient and formulate organizational strategies that look beyond the immediate fiscal year, or indeed, quarter.

The Japanese are no strangers to avoidance themselves, but their emphasis on performance in the long run takes pressure off managers. Not surprisingly, Japanese executives live healthier, saner, and longer lives than their American counterparts. Our managers pay a high price indeed for the highly stressed lives that they are forced to lead.

While heavy organizational pressure to perform is at least a partial explanation for the lingering presence of authoritarian managerial practices, another part of the answer may again be found in the psychology of personality development. A small percentage of individuals in our society, probably no more that 5 percent or so, fit a clinical personality pattern known as "authoritarianism." Authoritarian individuals are deeply disturbed persons who are attracted to positions of authority, and who persistently abuse any authority they are given.[3]

These individuals abuse authority precisely because *they* have been abused by authority figures, most often parents. The neighborhood bully is an authoritarian stereotype. The bully is always an older, stronger child who takes perverse delight in physically abusing younger, weaker children. While the bully remains a figure of contempt for those of us who suffered at his hands, when we look beyond our revulsion into the dynamics of his home, we find a disturbingly familiar pattern. The bully frequently is himself a victim of a punitive and abusive parent.

Authoritarian personalities are much attracted to the field of law enforcement, and sophisticated modern police departments go to expensive lengths to screen them out before they enter or complete training. In police parlance, they are known as "bad cops" because when they escape detection and find themselves armed and in uniform, they engage in violent behaviors that make every police chief in America shudder. It is a tribute to the professionalism of our major law-enforcement agencies that so few of them find their way into police work.

It is comforting to conclude this discussion of tough-guy management with a reference to our well-justified historical suspicion of authority and its abuse. "Power corrupts and absolute power corrupts absolutely," Lord Acton once said, and in our democracy we have recognized that fact empirically by creating a system of checks and balances at virtually every level in society that makes long-term abuse of power and authority very difficult. Even if authoritarian managers are not checked by other means, their flouting of accepted principles of fair play and due process soon leads to their downfall.

An Alternative to Nice-Guy and Tough-Guy Managerial Extremes

Fortunately, there is an alternative to the nice-guy and tough-guy approaches to solving problems that lies mid-way between them on the continuum of managerial authority (refer back to Figure 1). The remainder of this volume is devoted to discussing this alternative, the tough-minded approach,[4] which is a problem-solving managerial model. Because this model is a direct outgrowth of two decades of consulting experience, a lot of which was spent helping private- and public-sector managers deal with problem employees and the headaches they create for management, it focuses initially on problem-employee situations and is then generalized to deal with other problems managers face. It is unashamedly practical but has respectable theoretical roots. It is designed to help the reader and the managerial practitioner take effective action to deal with problems before they lead to chronic trauma for everyone involved.

Tough-minded managerial problem solving has the following general characteristics.

1. It deals with problems now, rather than later.
2. It can be used by managers at any level in any organization.
3. Its basic techniques can easily be learned by anyone.
4. It will almost immediately increase the manager's sense of self-esteem, reduce feelings of guilt and inadequacy, and improve his general outlook greatly.

It is interesting to note that while research shows that new managers are extremely anxious about effective disciplinary procedures and coping with employee problems generally, business schools only infrequently offer courses or seminars in this area. Most of the training being done nationally is being carried out in-house by government and industry, in response to real and pressing needs, or by consulting firms that have identified a growing market niche for such training.

The model described here has been developed over a 15-year period, is highly empirical, and has been used to train some 1,500 supervisors in both the public and private sectors. An equal number of undergraduate and graduate business majors have also been exposed to it. Managers who have used it report that it has consistently helped them deal with problem employees and problem situations more effectively. There are five almost equally important steps in tough-minded managerial problem solving:

1. Resolving to take action and setting up a good interview;
2. Stating the problem in an objective, specific, nonblaming, matter-of-fact way;
3. Giving the employee a fair hearing, and learning more about the problem;
4. Getting a promise of action from the employee that will solve the problem; and
5. Learning to document problem situations and follow up on actions taken.

Careful and effective use of this sequence of steps will almost always prevent the sort of screaming confrontations that no manager likes, and most dread. Most problem situations can be resolved successfully without formal disciplinary action or termination, and it is the major goal of this slender volume to teach managers everywhere how to achieve this result.

A CONSTRUCTIVE DIALOGUE

Let's stop for a minute and look at a problem situation. The following dialogue illustrates that the tough-guy approach is sometimes too aggressive to achieve results, while the tough-minded approach allows everyone involved to maintain their self-respect.

"Douglas the Drowsy Student"

As Professor John Briar walked into his classroom, bursting with his customary vigor, and prepared to lecture to his 9:00 A.M. Introductory Marketing class, an unusual sight caught his eye. Sprawled on top of a front-row table with his head down and obviously asleep, was Douglas Anderson, the star running back of the Acme College national championship football team. Other students were sneaking sympathetic glances at the slumbering Anderson, who was oblivious to all activities in the classroom.

Briar, a retired Army major and strict disciplinarian, was not amused. "Anderson," he bellowed, "Get your lazy butt off that table, and get your worthless body out of this room. You can come back to class after you've swung by my office and apologized for this. Now get moving."

Anderson woke with a start, rubbed his eyes, and sheepishly left the room. The other students looked studiously at their desk tops and pretended that he did not exist. Briar charged ahead with the lecture.

The following afternoon Professor Briar received a written message from the Acme College staff physician: "Please excuse Douglas Anderson from class for an indefinite period, due to illness." As he read the message, he made a mental note to talk to young Anderson when he reappeared in class.

Three weeks later, Briar heard a knock on his office door, and he called out, "Come in." The door opened, and Douglas Anderson entered the office:

Briar: Well, young man, good to see you back on campus. How are you feeling? I got a note from Dr. Walker that you were ill. Hope it was nothing too serious.

Anderson: Oh, well thank you sir. I'm feeling fine now. I'm glad Doc Walker sent you a note, because I had kind of a bad case of mono, and I didn't know it. I'd been feeling real punk for a couple of weeks before that morning in your class—just feeling real tired, and run-down—but that morning was the worst. I really want to apologize to you sir, for falling asleep and all, but I just couldn't keep my eyes open. And I usually really enjoy your lectures. No kidding.

Briar: Thanks, Douglas, but there's no need to apologize, now that I know what happened. In fact, I think I owe you an apology for yelling at you the way I did. I guess I assumed you had a bad hangover from a fraternity party, or something like that.

Anderson: Well, that's been known to happen at this College, sir, but that wasn't the case this time, I can assure you.

Briar: Well, obviously it wasn't, Douglas, and I appreciate it that you were responsible enough to come in and see me. You've always been a good student, and it was unusual to see you sound asleep like that. Let's talk about some make-up work you can do to make up for the time you lost while you were sick. Sound O.K. to you?

Anderson: Sounds great to me, sir. Thanks for giving me a chance to stay in the course.

Two months later, Douglas Anderson opened the envelope containing his spring semester grades and noted with pride that Professor Briar had given him a final grade of "A" in Introductory Marketing.

ENDNOTES

1. Albert Speer, *Inside the Third Reich* (New York: MacMillan, 1970).

2. Rensis Likert, *The Human Organization: Its Management and Value* (New York: McGraw-Hill, 1967): 78–100.

3. T. W. Adorno, et. al., *The Authoritarian Personality: Studies in Prejudice* (New York: Harper and Row, 1950).

4. The term "tough-minded management" was first used by management consultant Joe Batten, in *Tough-Minded Management* (New York: American Management Association, 1963). Although it is used and developed in a somewhat different context in this volume, it is

readily acknowledged by the author that the basic concepts described here have been known to good managers not only for decades, but for centuries.

Nice-Guy Lesson #3

**Two wrongs don't make a right—
Nice guy vs. Tough guy**

TOUGH-MINDED MANAGEMENT
GETS THE JOB DONE

The Power of a Preventive Policy

"An ounce of prevention is worth a pound of cure," advises an ancient proverb, and nowhere is this more true than when it comes to effectively using clear and well-communicated personnel policies to prevent problem-employee situations from developing or getting worse. Employers in industries such as construction, trucking, and timber, to name a few where drug and alcohol abuse have historically been widespread, are discovering that effective communication of anti-drug and alcohol policies can reduce substance abuse in the workplace by more than 50 percent. The resulting savings in reduced absenteeism, improved productivity, and fewer formal disciplinary actions may be difficult to calculate in actual dollars but these savings are so significant that intelligent employers readily recognize their value.

Preventive personnel policies, to be effective, require two distinct supervisory steps: (1) clear communication of the policy at the time of hiring, and (2) highly visible posting of the policy throughout the workplace. Step 1 requires that each new employee be briefed verbally during the initial personnel orientation session, and also be given a written statement of the policy in the employee handbook. In addition to a verbal briefing, some employers require each new employee to sign a form stating that they have read, and understand, the organization's policies on drug and alcohol abuse; and that their understanding includes an awareness of what the disciplinary consequences will be if they are found to be in violation of those policies.

Visible or public posting of substance-abuse policies means just that, of course. Employers in the construction industry find

it effective to post large printed signs, with bold and brightly colored lettering, at visible locations throughout a construction site. Fences, walls, posts, and washroom areas are excellent locations for such signs. While sign wording varies from employer to employer, wording similar to the following is recommended:

"WARNING: CONSUMPTION OF ALCOHOL OR ANY CONTROLLED SUBSTANCE ON THIS CONSTRUCTION SITE WILL BE GROUNDS FOR IMMEDIATE TERMINATION."

A word to the wise for the interested employer: Check with the legal department before launching any such policy. While the steps that have just been described are clear and legal, in the hands of an overly enthusiastic or tough-guy supervisor, they can easily be abused, and viewed in a formal legal proceeding as a form of harassment.

Legal issues aside for a moment, it makes good managerial and human-relations sense during an initial communications session to explain exactly *why* the organization has implemented such a policy, e.g., "Consuming alcohol or drugs on a construction site poses a real safety hazard not only to the employee who has consumed such substances, but to other employees as well." As usual, the tough-minded problem-solving rule here is to treat employees as adults, which means with courtesy and respect.

Chapter 4

RESOLVING TO TAKE ACTION AND SETTING UP THE INTERVIEW

You are the supervisor of an auditing group with the Internal Revenue Service, and one of your new employees, Mary Ellen Reilly, has just come to you with a complaint. She states that while she was standing at the water cooler a few minutes ago, one of your junior auditors, Lowell Loveless, pinched her as she was getting a cup of water. She says she is extremely angry and upset and that she in no way encouraged his advances. Lowell has worked under your supervision for three years and has been a satisfactory employee. He is married and has three children. During the last year, you have heard rumors in the office that he has made advances toward several of the female employees.

You decide to interview him regarding Ms. Reilly's complaint.[1]

The Decision to Take Action

As you sit at your desk, reflecting on what Mary Ellen Reilly has just told you, you begin to break out in a sweat. You realize that she is extremely upset, and that if nothing is done about the situation, she is likely to file a sexual harassment complaint. You suspect that Loveless, the junior auditor, is guilty as charged; after all, there have been rumors swirling about the office, and where there's smoke, there's usually fire. Besides, the man's manner is bold and flirtatious and not only that, he favors brightly colored shirts with paisley ties and wears a heavily perfumed cologne.

You are miserable. You know you need to do something. Yet this is a delicate and embarrassing situation. If you talk to him about Mary's complaint, you will be intruding in a highly personal and sensitive matter. The man probably has some complex sexual hang-up or other problem that will require the help of someone like Dr. Ruth. You could just make matters worse if you interview him and screw up. Anyway, if you talk to him about something like this, he's just going to fly off the handle and scream at you. Maybe if you just talk to Mary again and ask her to stay away from him for awhile, the whole thing will blow over, and maybe you can talk to him in a week or two when things have cooled off. That's it, talk to him in a few weeks.

And then you realize that you are kidding yourself, doing a little mental judo that will leave you tied in knots, leave you feeling ashamed of yourself and unwilling to look Mary in the eye. The situation's gone too far and the time has come to do something. You decide to interview Lowell at 10:00 the following morning and to go home this evening and plan how you're going to handle the meeting.

In the slightly melodramatic account of a manager's decision-making process that you have just read, you have witnessed a familiar interplay: the conflict between the supervisor's adult and rational knowledge that there is a problem situation that needs to be dealt with, now, and the all-too familiar desire to avoid the conflict that may result if action is taken. There is probably no single factor in a manager's decision to do something to solve a problem, but there are some positive pressures that result in action.

One factor is the sure knowledge that matters will only get worse if nothing is done. A second is the desire to maintain one's own respect, as well as the respect of employees. A third is the desire to maintain a harmonious and productive work environment, where people can work hard and well without fear of harassment. And the fourth factor is the knowledge that there are many skills and techniques available that will resolve this problem quickly and informally, long before it becomes a legalistic nightmare.

Perhaps it is this last point that should be emphasized and re-emphasized: When a manager feels that he or she knows *what* to do about a problem and also feels confident that he or she can effectively use *skills* and *techniques* to resolve it, then decisive action is much more likely to follow. Nothing is more discouraging than to hear a manager say, "I knew that I should do something. I knew it was a real problem, but I really didn't have a clue what to do." In some cases, a statement like this might be just another cop-out, but all too often it has the plaintive ring of truth. Most supervisors have simply had no training in what to do about problems like the one we have just encountered.

Another impetus to action lies again in the realm of rational and adult thinking, and that is the knowledge that the manager not only has a right, but has an *obligation,* to take action when any problem surfaces that affects performance; that is, any problem that in any way prevents the job from getting done. Many employees are also into avoidance, understandably, and this is never more true than in the situation where employees have simply never seen effective managerial action taken to solve a problem. In a sexual harassment case, the employee might not say anything at all to her supervisor, firstly because she fears nothing will be done, and secondly because she is afraid that there will be retaliation against her if she complains.

If the employee does have the courage to come forward, the complaint might also be followed by a statement like, "But please don't tell Mr. Loveless that I complained. Please don't use my name." In a familiar real-world case like this, the manager can continue practicing avoidance ("Well gosh, then I guess there's nothing we can do.") or begin using tough-minded skills to solve the problem. The manager can begin taking effective action at this point by saying, "Mary, I want to take action about your complaint, and I will, but I'm not going to be able to do anything effective about it if you won't let me use your name. I can understand that you might be a bit afraid to let me do that, but if your concern is that Lowell is going to retaliate against you in some way, believe me, that's the last thing that's going to happen."

Let's take a moment to discuss and understand both the manager's statement and the employee's fear in this instance. By making the statement in the way he did, the manager is not only asserting that he will indeed take action, he is giving the employee encouragement and support for coming forward. He is also making what psychologists might call a reality input. After he has interviewed Mr. Loveless about the employee's complaint, irrespective of what actually happened at the water

49

cooler, retaliation against her will be about the last thing on Loveless's mind. His first priority, as we shall see, will be to take action to resolve the problem. His most likely future behavior toward her, whether he pinched her or not, will be to stay away from her. There will be no more physical contact.

A final rational guide to managerial action that is particularly useful in bringing down the barrier of guilt is the knowledge that by taking tough-minded action, the manager is actually acting as a friend toward the problem employee. This notion at first appears inherently contradictory because our conventional notion of discipline is punitive. Tough-minded discipline is nothing of the sort. The employee is treated as a self-respecting adult, and discipline takes the form of feedback to the employee about the nature of the problem. The motivation to solve the problem is not so much the employee's fear of being punished or losing his job as it is his desire to keep his manager's respect.

But acting as a friend? Sure. By bringing the problem to the employee's attention now, and by giving him a chance to take action to resolve it, the manager is giving the employee a chance to avoid further complaints, formal disciplinary action (which *is* punitive), and the possible loss of his job. By doing nothing, the problem situation will grow worse, and ultimately there may be no alternative but a tough-guy firing. Hiding the existence of a problem from an employee or failing to bring a problem to the employee's attention is a real disservice to the employee.

It is perhaps the implicit recognition of this truth that magnifies the agonized guilt of the nice-guy manager. The first emotion that most managers experience when they make the courageous decision to take action is a tremendous sense of relief: "It felt so good just to know that I was *doing* something" is a common statement. Relief is almost always accompanied, not surprisingly, by a renewed sense of pride and self-esteem in one's capabilities and courage.

Let's Not Pretend This Is Fun

In this discussion of taking action to solve a problem situation, no attempt has been made to imply that such a decision is ever easy, or that effectively interviewing a problem employee is ever fun. Such a pretense would be dishonest. Intervening in a problem-employee situation is one of the toughest things a manager can do, even if the rewards are well worth it. Even the most effective and courageous managers report that they typically agonize about the decision to take action, they feel uncomfortable during the interview itself, and they are glad when it's over.

The desire for honesty, however, is a powerful one. When lying behavior, as we have already noted, is replaced by honesty, the increase in the self-esteem of the individual is remarkable. Any person practicing avoidance is lying to himself a lot and at bottom he always knows it. Real courage has never consisted of whistling in the dark. It has more to do with doing something effective even when one is shaking inside and knowing that the psychic payoff will be worth it.

Setting up the Interview

Once the decision has been made to meet the employee one on one and face to face (no letters or memos please), practical arrangements need to be made to set up the interview. The fastest way to set up the interview is normally to give the employee a call, and in a matter-of-fact manner ask him if he would mind coming down to the manager's office for a few minutes. The general rule here is to be calm, understated, and courteous. The employee should be *asked*, not told, to come in for an interview.

The tough-guy manager will immediately put the employee on the defensive by calling him or leaning over his desk and barking, "Smith, get down to my office right away, I want to talk to you." Poor Smith will realize immediately that it is not instant-coffee time. The nice-guy manager will heighten the employee's anxiety by sending him an elaborate memorandum asking for a "conference" at a set time some weeks in the future.

Once the employee arrives in the manager's office, somewhat apprehensively, the tough-guy manager will immediately engage in intimidating power games. One tactic that is sure to leave the employee feeling weak and vulnerable is for the manager to stand behind his desk, complete with American flag and bald eagle, point to a chair that has been strategically placed in the middle of the room (or, as the employee perceives it, in the middle of the Pacific ocean with no canoe available), and sternly thunder, "Fred, have a chair." In the employee's mind, after detecting all of the symbols of great managerial authority, a pistol whipping is bound to follow.[2]

The nice-guy manager can put the employee equally on the defensive by falling all over the person as he enters the manager's office, thumping him heartily on the back and saying, "Fred, it's so good to see you. How are you buddy? Boy, it's a beautiful day. How are Edna and the kids? How's every little thing with you, big guy?" The message that is conveyed here by the manager, who disguises with phony congeniality his unease at actually having the employee physically present, is that something's up, something probably not good. Most employees can detect insincerity, and when they do, they assume the worst.

False praise leading into the interview is another chickenshit nice-guy tactic that makes things worse. If the problem person has just been told that he's the "best worker we've ever had around here," and he knows full well that he's just messed up six straight lab tests, his antennae will be twitching nervously. Far better to maintain a low-key, calm, and courteous style, with a polite request to the employee phrased something like, "Would you like to have a chair, Joe?"

Seating the employee at a corner of a desk, if one is available, is a recommended tactic, because it allows for a face-to-face conversation, without recourse to symbols of power that carry a connotation of punishment, and also allows both persons the security of having something to lean on or touch during the interview. When the employee gets the supervisor's call requesting a meeting, the first question that will occur to him is "why?" followed by apprehension that the meeting has to do with a problem, and he will arrive in something approaching a state of free-floating anxiety. Courteous, low-key treatment will help calm things and get the interview off to a better start.

A question supervisors often ask in this connection is, "What should I tell the person if he asks me why I want to see him?" A basic tough-minded rule should be followed here: Don't lie and don't imply that a social chit-chat is what's in store. The manager can say something like, "There's a bit of a problem we need to talk about, which I think we can clear up pretty quickly." In this situation, some anxiety simply cannot be avoided, and the directness of the supervisor's response lets the employee know that it's going to be a problem-solving meeting, but that a constructive outcome is anticipated.

A short note here that may seem almost too commonsensical: Hold the interview in private. Even if the manager does not have an office, a place that affords privacy can almost certainly be found, even though many modern American buildings and homes are not well designed from this point of view. Public interviews produce paranoia and extreme defensiveness, not surprisingly. They are favored by tough guys because the employee can be humiliated publicly by his macho boss. They are not used by managers who are seeking long-term solutions to problems.

How Not to Fall into the Small-Talk Trap

Many training manuals recommend a short period of small talk after the employee has been seated and prior to the interview itself. The purpose of a period of small talk is worthy. It can serve to relax the person, get him talking, and convey the nonverbal message that he's not here to be punished. While small talk can often accomplish just what it's supposed to, it can also become yet another trap for the nice-guy manager to fall into.

Because the nice guy really doesn't want to deal with the problem, the period of small talk becomes intensely absorbing. The manager asks question after question about Fred's latest fishing trip or his current home-remodeling project. After 30 minutes of such pleasantries, the manager glances at his watch and announces, "Oh my goodness, I'm late for a meeting. We'll just have to get together again." The employee leaves feeling either confused or amused. Amusement is more likely, because most people are bright enough to recognize yet another cop-out. The manager leaves still squirming with anxiety, knowing full well that his chickenshit behaviors have done him in again, but vowing to take action "soon."

Small talk can be used effectively by the tough-minded manager. There are two very basic and sensible rules to follow: (1) Plan exactly what small talk to make, and (2) plan how long it will last. Small talk that is work-related is generally most effective. The employee can be asked a relevant question such as,

"How's the audit going?" that allows him to respond relatively freely with words of his own choosing. If the answer is something like, "Fine," followed by nothing, the manager might follow up with another query such as, "Good to hear. Do you have an expected completion date yet?" Just a question or two, with no phony praise. Just a minute or so, and then on to the interview itself.

A final thought on small talk for the manager. If the planned small talk seems contrived or phony, or if the manager is simply eager to get on with the interview, then dispense with it. There are so many avenues of avoidance that there is no sense in creating the temptation to follow another one to the detriment of effective and tough-minded problem solving. There probably are times, in the good judgment of the supervisor, when almost any period of small talk would distract from dealing with the problem, and if that is his considered judgment, he should follow his own counsel.

Why the One-on-One Interview

The inquisitive reader may well ask at this point why the one-on-one interview is being stressed so heavily as a medium for problem solving. At the risk of sounding a trifle flip, the answer is that most human problems are solved one on one, face to face. Direct communication with the employee is the most powerful single tool the manager has available to deal with problem situations, including performance problems.

Perhaps this point can be effectively illustrated in the negative, by reminding readers of a group-based chickenshit cop-out that has enraged generations of American schoolchildren. This is, of course, the case of the gutless teacher punishing the entire class because she didn't have the nerve to discipline the mayor's son, who everyone knew had stolen little Linda's lunch bucket. Is there a one of us who was not exposed to this classic maneuver? Who did not sit impatiently in his desk hating both the teacher and the mayor's larcenous offspring?

Perhaps the one good thing that can be said about group punishment is that it will sometimes motivate the group to take effective action to make sure that lunch-bucket theft does not occur again. In adult work environments, when the nonperforming employee is given unsubtle signals by his workmates that they don't appreciate his transgressions, he will often shape up. Even though this may relieve the manager from immediate responsibility for taking action, his respect is still not enhanced in the eyes of his employees, who always recognize gutlessness when they see it.

Knowing When the Time Has Come to Take Action

A very practical question that often arises in training sessions is when the manager should take action in a problem-employee situation. How many times should he or she wait, for example, for a tardy employee to come in late before talking to that person? While no definitive answer can be given, there are two considerations that seem to satisfy the criterion of "common sense."*

The first is that it is far better to move early than late. In the case of a tardy employee, the second absence in a one-week to one-month time period would certainly justify a short interview. In general, whenever there is a departure from what is considered a satisfactory performance standard, there is justification for action. In many organizations, clearly stated performance policies and procedures make the supervisor's life much easier. If the attendance policy states that an interview with a manager is required after any two absences in a given period, there can be no question whatsoever of the right to intervene.

A second consideration is a more subjective, experiential one. It has to do with managerial discomfort, and it may be stated as follows: If the manager finds himself thinking of a problem employee or performance situation after hours, or feels a twinge of discomfort or unease about that person or situation as he is just driving along, the time has come to take action. When the manager begins dreaming in technicolor about the employee, then the time is well past to take action! Learning to trust one's guts, as it were, can be an excellent remedy for gutless behavior.

---

*The late Bertrand Russell, among other philosophers, once observed that there is nothing so extraordinarily uncommon as common sense.

STEP 1: TAKING ACTION
AND SETTING UP THE INTERVIEW

- *Resolve* to take action when the problem becomes apparent. Intervene *early*. The worst thing you can do is *nothing*.

- *Ask* for a meeting with the employee. Meet in *private*.

- *Ask* the employee to be seated. Sit face to face with no desk intervening.

- Be courteous to the employee, and treat him or her as an *adult*.

- Use a bit of *small talk*, if it seems natural and will relax the employee. If it doesn't, don't use it.

A CONSTRUCTIVE DIALOGUE

Let's stop for a minute and look at a problem-employee situation. The manager in the following incident recognized a problem, and took prompt, tough-minded action by meeting with the employee to resolve it.

"The Restaurateur"

Frances Smith was the founder, president, and full-time manager of the Lynch Street Regulars, Inc., a St. Louis restaurant. One of the more interesting employees of the restaurant was Dennis Adams, whom Frances had hired as a bus-boy and kitchen handyman a few months earlier. Dennis was a conscientious employee, performed the tasks his job required with a minimum of supervision, and kept the kitchen of the restaurant cleaner than had any previous employee. Unfortunately, Dennis also had a bit of a performance problem: He enjoyed stealing food from the kitchen. When Dennis was ready to empty the garbage, which was taken to a dumpster at the rear of the property, he would remove a ten-pound bag of frozen porterhouse steaks from the freezer (making sure that he was unobserved), and slide the bag of steaks under the lettuce and other produce scraps that he filled the garbage can with. As he approached the dumpster, he would deftly pull the bag of steaks out of the scraps of produce, toss it into the back of his truck (that he had carefully parked near the dumpster), and then empty the garbage.

Frances learned of all this because another employee had, unbeknownst to Dennis, seen him stealing a bag of steaks as she was leaving the employee washroom. She immediately notified Frances of what she had seen, and indignantly demanded, "What are you going to do about him, Mrs. Smith?" "Don't worry, Liz," Frances replied, "I'm going to nail him good." And she did.

A few days later, as she glanced into the kitchen she saw Dennis moving around near the garbage can, casually throwing scraps of garbage into it. Acting on the basis of a marvelously accurate intuition (sharpened by her observation that no steaks had disappeared for several days), she strode into the kitchen and in a firm voice said, "Wait just a minute, young man." Dennis froze. Frances marched up to the garbage can, reached in, and pulled out a slightly soggy bag of steaks. "What do you have to say for yourself?" she demanded.

Dennis said nothing, but seized a large butcher knife that was lying on a work table and took a step toward Frances. Although she was inwardly terrified, she retained her composure, and said to the menacing employee, "Dennis, if you cut me with the knife, you're going to do a long stretch in the federal pen. So think it over for a bit, will you. I think you'll be smart and put down the knife."

Dennis hesitated, lost his nerve, threw down the knife, and bolted out of the Lynch Street Regulars at a high rate of speed. He did not return to collect his final paycheck.

ENDNOTES

1. Developed and adapted from the author's consulting experience.

2. Michael Korda, *Power* (New York: Random House, 1976).

TOUGH-MINDED MANAGEMENT
GETS THE JOB DONE

What to Do When the *Boss* Is the Problem

Let us express some simple human sympathy for the employee who finds himself or herself working for a problem boss: Any boss, who for whatever reason, is not getting the job done; who is not solving problems, but is actually creating them or making them worse. The dilemma facing any employee in such a situation is truly painful: To cope with the problem is to risk termination, or at least some form of retaliation, and to take any action at all is likely to involve dealing with a very high level of fear. The employee who decides to do nothing, and seek employment elsewhere, will not be judged harshly in these pages.

Nonetheless, effective action can sometimes be taken, although the advice that follows is not offered as a "quick fix" or a panacea for dealing with the problem boss. Firstly, we might ask, what are some common problem-boss situations? Not surprisingly, these problems are very similar both in kind and degree to typical problem-employee situations.

1. The supervisor consistently avoids dealing with problem employees, thereby creating problems for all the other employees.
2. The supervisor has serious personal problems that interfere with or impede his or her job performance.
3. The supervisor is a classic "boss," which is to say, an authoritarian tough guy who intimidates, abuses, and alienates employees.
4. The supervisor fails to support employees in confrontations with other levels of management.
5. The supervisor is inconsistent, vacillates, or plays favorites among employees.

59

Nice-Guy Lesson #4

**Nice guys will often use small talk
to avoid the interview topic.**

6. The supervisor displays discriminatory attitudes or engages in discriminatory behavior toward members of sexual, racial, or ethnic groups.

While the preceding list of behaviors and situations engaged in or created by supervisors who are themselves problems is not intended to be either definitive or exhaustive, it does represent a reasonably complete laundry list of problems likely to be encountered by an employee. Because the power of authority in every society is much greater than we sometimes realize,* employees will normally feel very intimidated when they first encounter an abuse of authority, and will also feel powerless to do something about it. As we have already noted, *fear*—stifling, paralyzing, overwhelming, confusing fear—will also be a constant companion while attempts are being made to resolve the situation.

What can the average employee do, then, in one of these situations? When fears are strong, or when chickenshit managers at every level have successfully avoided coping with the problem, employees will sometimes resort to sneaky, underhanded, Machiavellian (and successful) strategies for solving the problem informally. While the author does not recommend or approve of these strategies because they are frequently unethical and even close to illegal, he nonetheless understands all too well the desperation of employees who use them.

A case in point occurred several years ago when the author was still active as a consultant to the United States Office of Personnel Management. It seems that Joe (all names have been changed to protect the guilty), who was the manager of a GSA office in a major Midwestern city, was a chronic drunk. He would normally report to work in the morning, sober, but would repair to a local tavern for a two-and-a-half hour lunch, after which he was largely dysfunctional during the afternoon hours. Top management had done nothing about Joe and his drinking problem despite frequent complaints from his employees about their boss's behavior, which had gone on for many years.

---

*The curious reader is referred to Stanley Milgram's book, *Obedience to Authority* (New York: Harper and Row, 1974), for a dramatic and gripping account of the startling obedience of a group of American adults to a verbal order to administer severe "electric shock" to an innocent person.

Finally, Joe's creative and highly frustrated employees took matters into their own hands. One afternoon, Joe (slightly inebriated as usual) magically and mysteriously tumbled from his chair as it crumbled beneath him, broke his hip, and was forced to take disability retirement. The authors of this "accident" confessed to the author of this volume that they had engineered the dramatic failure of Joe's chair by cunningly loosening some bolts, which they tightened after Joe had been carted away to a local emergency room. Such are the tales a consultant sometimes hears when he is touring the circuit. Many are true.

Employees can frequently take effective action that falls short of such overt sabotage, however. The basic technique recommended here, as you might expect, is the use of three steps of the tough-minded management process:

1. State the problem clearly and objectively to the supervisor;
2. Talk the problem through; and
3. Get a promise of action that will solve the problem.

Needless to say, the employee should also *document* every action that he or she takes in an attempt to solve the problem.

In the real world, it will of course be agonizingly painful for any employee to take such a step or steps. Fear is powerful and distorts judgment. Retaliation is possible, but is not *likely*, for all the reasons given earlier in this book. The normal supervisor will want to take action that reduces conflict with a disaffected employee or *group* of employees. This last comment suggests yet another powerful action step: If several employees are unhappy about a managerial situation, which is often the case, they will maximize their clout with management by confronting a supervisor or supervisors as a group. Again, constructive results are most likely if the group follows tough-minded problem-solving steps, and has a clear goal or outcome in mind. Such a goal orientation will help prevent the meeting from degenerating into a "bitching" session.

If a tough-minded meeting with the supervisor produces no results, the employee is more than justified in going up the organization (approaching persons at higher levels of authority in the organization) to solve the problem. This is a strategy that is more likely to be effective if the employee has already confronted the supervisor about the problem, and can document that he or she has done so. This reduces or removes the implication that the employee is merely "tattling," and is more likely to elicit a sympathetic human response.

All too often, however, top management is also part of the problem. The recent case of FBI Agent Donald Rochon is a good example. Rochon, who is black, complained of crude incidents of racial harassment while assigned to the Omaha, Nebraska office in 1983. "Pranks" on the level of having a photograph of his children defaced by having a picture of an ape pasted over their faces were the order of the day in Omaha. When Rochon complained bitterly to his superiors about such actions, they made light of the whole matter (characterizing it as "healthy," in one case), and took no formal action whatsoever to stop the harassment.

Rochon, who is no quitter, went formal with his case and won favorable rulings from both the Justice Department and the Equal Employment Opportunity Commission supporting his claim of discrimination and harassment. In numerous media appearances, Agent Rochon made an eloquent and ironic point: The very agency charged with enforcing the nation's civil rights laws was in fact flagrantly violating them. His personal courage in pursuing his case must be applauded by all, and illustrates clearly how one gutsy and determined individual can effectively confront a sea of injustice and gutlessness.

Chapter 5

SOLVING THE PROBLEM BY SIMPLY STATING IT

There is an ancient Indian pictorial joke, told in two boxes. The good reader will supply his or her own visualizations. Box 1: Two gentlemen wearing turbans are seated on the back of a large elephant. In the distance, another beturbaned gentleman is seen pointing at the elephant, saying, "Look at the two assholes on that elephant!" Box 2: The two gentlemen who were previously seated atop the elephant are now seen standing at the rear of the beast, holding up its tail and looking curiously thereunder.

If there is one magical and critical moment in tough-minded problem solving that is at once exquisitely simple and terribly difficult, it is stating the problem situation to the employee simply and objectively. If the problem can be stated calmly in this way by a determined manager, without accompanying statements and nonverbal behaviors that judge or accuse the employee, about 75 to 80 percent of all problem situations will already have taken a giant leap toward resolution. Since this assertion has dogmatic overtones, and the skeptical reader will immediately be inclined to ask why, it would be wise to examine closely why a carefully worded problem statement can have a powerful impact on behavior and be a powerful problem-solving tool.

Firstly, let us examine the characteristics of an effective, tough-minded problem statement. The continuing example of the amorous auditor will serve to illustrate the point:

Supervisor: Lowell, you're probably wondering why I asked you to come on in and talk with me today. Well, the reason is that Mary Reilly, the new girl in your unit, came by my office yesterday afternoon, and she stated that while she was standing by the water cooler, at about three o'clock, she said you came down the aisle next to the cooler, and pinched her. She said she was very upset about it and asked me to talk to you about it. Could you tell me what happened or what you remember about that?

In this case, the manager has truly bitten the bullet, and problem solving is about to occur. The employee has now been made aware of the problem situation, and without histrionics. Names, times, dates, and places have been given, but in a non-accusatory manner. The employee has been told some critically important things and has been motivated to solve the problem, without once having been told overtly. What things have been communicated implicitly? At least seven things have been communicated that will have a positive impact on the problem.

1. I am your boss.
2. I am going to take action to solve this problem.
3. You are now responsible for taking some action that will help solve this problem.
4. If you don't take some action that will help solve the problem, irrespective of who did what to whom, there's trouble down the road.
5. I'm not here to judge you or to punish you, but I want to see this problem solved.
6. Pinching or sexual harassment, if it occurred, is not acceptable behavior in this organization.
7. I'm willing to hear you talk about the problem.

There is an old cliché about things not said being just as important as things that are, and in the case of the problem statement, this was never more true. Almost all of these messages, if they had been communicated verbally to the employee, however nicely, would offend him and immediately put him on the defensive. If the supervisor were so unwise as to say, "You know, I'm your boss," the employee might well make the following interpretations of this all-too-frequent foot-in-the-mouth statement:

1. I'm a child being talked to by an adult.
2. I'm too stupid to know who my own boss is.
3. My boss is a pretty insecure individual to have to tell me that.
4. I'm here to be bossed around (i.e., punished).

Some Do's and Don'ts in Phrasing the Problem Statement

Choosing the exact wording or phrasing of the statement of the problem, including the exact tone of voice and appropriate body language to use, is of such importance in getting action from the employee that it is well worth rehearsing and practicing before the interview itself takes place. Practice and rehearsal are a good way to help control the nervousness that the manager is bound to feel during the interview, particularly at the moment the transition from small talk to problem statement takes place.

The manager is not expected to be a thespian, and it may seem a little silly for a grown-up person to sit quietly in his or her office saying, "Now, I'm going to say in a calm voice—not speaking too quickly—'Lowell, you're probably wondering . . . ,' " but the results will usually be worth it. As we shall soon be seeing, the English language is so full of "loaded" words that will immediately put the employee on the defensive, that it is hard to avoid (in a good sense) using at least some of them.

In wording the problem statement, there are several important "do's." The first is to word the statement in terms of the performance problem, without using that term, which to the average individual is something of a turn-off because of its slightly pompous overtones. "The performance problem we're here to discuss, Joe, . . . ," has a slightly ominous ring, as if a nuclear holocaust might be around the corner. In the continuing saga of Mr. Loveless, the performance problem is simply that one employee has made a complaint about the behavior of another.

A second "do" is to be completely and absolutely specific. Don't beat around the bush. In the example at the outset of the chapter, once the supervisor has finished his statement, the employee knows exactly what the problem is. He doesn't have to guess about the nature of the complaint, or why he's in his supervisor's office. There is no longer any uncertainty about why the interview is taking place. Vague, circuitous statements, such as, "It's come to my attention that an incident of harassment may have occurred recently in our working environment," simply heighten anxiety.

A third important thing for the manager to do is to have all the facts assembled, to get them as straight as possible, and to incorporate key facts into the problem statement. In the case of tardiness, if employees are required to punch in (a bit of an anachronism in the contemporary workplace), the supervisor should have time cards available and on his desk covering the period in question. If time cards are not used, but the manager has made an anecdotal record of the employee's arrival times on the back of an envelope or on a note pad, then this record should also be on hand.

A key purpose of getting the facts together is to let the employee know that the manager is serious about dealing with the problem, again without having to say it. Another purpose is to head off an argument, for once the employee has succeeded in luring the unwary supervisor into a lengthy dispute over the facts of the matter, effective problem solving will not take place. This is a point that will be returned to again. If an adversary relationship develops during the interview, the manager will probably end up assuming a tough-guy role and screaming insults at the employee. Far better to terminate the interview for a while, and begin again a bit later, if this occurs.

After the problem itself has been identified, the manager should close the statement with an open-ended question such as, "Could you tell me what happened?" Questions that are genuinely open-ended are nonjudgmental, and make no presuppositions about what happened in the incident under discussion. This is another point that will be returned to at length, but learning to ask nonjudgmental questions is a bit trickier than it might at first seem.

If the manager closes the statement with a question like, "Now, I'd like to hear your side of the story, so could you tell me what happened?," he or she will have already put the employee on the defensive. "Your side of the story" is one of those loaded English phrases that implies that a legal proceeding is about to take place, and worse, that the employee is already behind the eight ball because his side of the story might not quite stack up. As the legendary hunter discovered, it is remarkably easy to shoot oneself right in the foot, and even a casual slip into judgmental language can undo an otherwise splendid opening to the interview.

Thus, there exists the need for rehearsal and careful selection of neutral, nonaccusatory phrases. In our ongoing example, the manager was careful to say that Ms. Reilly "stated" that Mr. Loveless pinched her. The manager didn't use words like "alleged" or even "accused," both of which have strong loadings. The combination of careful choice of words, calm manner, and open-ended conclusion made it a highly effective opening to the interview. The employee has been told exactly what the problem is and has also been told that he is free to talk about it without having been prejudged.

Some of the "don'ts" in phrasing the problem statement have already emerged in our discussion of "do's." The perceptive reader will long ago have identified the underlying theme. Stay away from judgmental, accusatory, blaming statements. Stay calm and don't act as though the sky is about to fall in. All of us seem to have a certain fascination with the Chicken Little Syndrome, but it doesn't help a problem-solving interview. The goal of the problem-statement phase of the interview is not to have the employee thinking in a panicky way, "Oh my God, it's the end of the world," but rather to have him thinking clearly and soberly, "There's a problem here, and I have responsibility for doing something about it."

Management by Rumor

One of the facts of life in any organizational environment is that there is an active informal communications network, sometimes better known as the rumor mill or grapevine. Rumors are never so abundant as they are during the great office love affair (the lovers always assume that no one in the office is privy to their guilty secret, and behave ever so discreetly, which heightens everyone else's enjoyment of their liaison since, of course, everyone else knows about it) or when there is a chronic problem-employee situation present. Inevitably and rapidly, these rumors will reach the ears of the manager.

Should the manager take action when he hears such rumors? The answer, in two words, is "definitely no." When the manager acts on the basis of a rumor, he immediately gives it credence, whether it's true or false. The employee who is confronted with a rumor will quite rightly assume that he has been prejudged and will respond in a predictably defensive manner. The old saying that where there's smoke, there's fire is sometimes true, of course; but often, where there's smoke, there's smoke.

Often an employee will come to the supervisor with a rumor, breathlessly saying something like, "Did you hear that Lowell Loveless pinched Mary Reilly while she was standing by the water cooler, and she's really upset. What are you going to do about it?" The appropriate answer for the tough-minded manager is something like, "I'm sorry to hear that, but I can't take action based on a rumor. Now, if Mary Reilly has a complaint, if she'll just come to me with it, then I can do something." A specific complaint always gives the manager a good reason to act. Acting on the basis of a rumor, however, is another good way to shoot oneself in the foot.

A Note on the Implicit Messages in the Problem Statement

Earlier in the chapter, it was noted that the tough-minded problem statement conveys a number of other implicit messages to the employee. Several of these are worth commenting on in somewhat more detail, beginning with the message, "I am your boss." This message is conveyed by the fact that the employee has been called in for the interview by the manager, but it is softened by the message that the employee is going to have a chance to talk about the problem to a friendly, helpful person who wants to see the problem solved.

The employee will have been powerfully motivated to do something to solve the problem after hearing it stated and will also feel responsible for doing something, irrespective of the actual cause of the problem. The average employee would usually rather keep his job than lose it, and he is almost always

STEP 2: SOLVING THE PROBLEM BY STATING IT EFFECTIVELY

- State the problem *specifically, objectively,* and *factually.* Don't beat around the bush.

- *Rehearse* what you're going to say and how you're going to say it because you're going to feel *nervous.*

- Review your list of *don'ts*: Don't preach, don't accuse, don't tell the employee you're the boss, and don't attempt to intimidate.

- Be as *calm* and *matter of fact* as you possibly can.

- End your statement with an *open-ended* question to get the employee talking.

bright enough to realize immediately that if he doesn't begin doing something, ultimately formal disciplinary action is going to be taken. He will also be motivated by a desire to maintain the respect of a manager who is being both highly professional and helpful. This positive motivation may be more meaningful to many employees than the prospect of trouble.

The shifting of responsibility to the employee is important because it leads smoothly into the next, or third phase of effective managerial problem solving: giving the employee a hearing and clarifying the problem.

A CONSTRUCTIVE DIALOGUE

Let's stop for a minute and consider the dangers of acting on rumors and gossip. The following dialogue illustrates that a manager needs to find out all the facts before acting on what could be a false rumor.

"The Tattletale"

Richard Carlyle managed the Publications Department of the Midwestern Agricultural Service Company in Kansas City, Missouri. His secretary, Donna Richland, had worked for him for more than three years and had been an excellent employee. Because he depended heavily on her to quickly and accurately process highly technical publications, he was concerned about maintaining a good relationship with her, and they often conversed about personal matters.

Recently, Donna had made him aware that she was having serious marital problems. While her job performance continued to be excellent, she often looked worried and tired, and Richard's heart went out to her. One Friday evening she looked so distraught that he impulsively said to her, "Hey kid, let's go out and grab a drink. You really look down." They left the office together at 5:00 P.M., and drove together in Richard's car to a nearby tavern where they each had three drinks. At 6:30 P.M., they returned to Midwestern's parking lot. Donna thanked Richard for taking the time to talk with her about her problem, kissed him on the cheek, got into her car, and drove off.

Through an office window, Marvin Nordstrom, another department manager, watched. Nordstrom then headed down the hall to the office of J. Robert Harper, the president of Midwestern, who was still working. "J.R., there's something I really think you oughtta know," Marvin began.

"What's that Marvin?" J.R. asked, without looking up from the report he was reading.

Marvin replied, "Well, J.R., I think there's a certain standard of conduct we expect from department managers here at Midwestern, and we're certainly not getting it in the Publications Department."

J.R. abruptly looked up from his report and asked, "What are you talking about, Marvin?"

Marvin: I'm talking about the hanky-panky that's been going on between Richard Carlyle and his secretary, that's what. Everyone's talking about it, the affair they're having. She's separated from her husband, and she's been going out with the boss. I just saw them smooching and snuggling out in the parking lot. They'd been out together drinking again, I suppose. God, it's disgusting.

J.R.: You mean they're getting it on. Is everyone talking?

Marvin: You'd better believe it. You should see them making eyes at each other. This is the kind of stuff we don't need at a company like Midwestern.

J.R.: I see what you mean, Marvin. I'm going to talk to Richard on Monday morning.

The following Monday, J.R. Harper wasted no time. He called Richard Carlyle at 8:00 A.M. and asked him to his office "immediately!" As Richard entered J.R.'s office a few minutes later, he said, "Hi Boss. What are you all fired up about?"

J.R.: Now Richard, doggone it, there's something we've got to talk about. As you know, we've got to have certain standards here at Midwestern, you know what I mean? I mean, we just can't have people, and particularly department managers, just running off and doing whatever they please.

Richard: J.R., I'm sorry, but I just don't have a clue in the world what you mean. With all due respect, could you come to the point?

J.R.: Well now Richard, this is a sensitive point, I'm sure, but it has come to my attention through a reliable source that you and Donna Richland are having a, well, love affair, and it's gotta stop. Now I'm not telling you how to conduct your personal life, Richard, but everyone's been talking about what's been going on, and it's really become a problem. So I'm asking you not to see her anymore, and not only that, to get a new secretary. Pronto.

Richard: Now hold on, J.R. I can't believe what you just said. I hate to say it, but I'm furious. For one thing, there's absolutely nothing going on between Donna and me, although apparently some damned tattletale has been running up to you behind my back and telling you this kind of crap. What really hurts is that you apparently believe it.

J.R.: Well, Richard, now I didn't say that, that I believe it. I'm just worried about what's good for the company. I can see you're real upset.

Richard: Well, damn it, J.R., I am. There's apparently been all this gossip going on behind my back. Donna's going through a bad situation with her husband, and I've been encouraging her to tell me about it, just to help her a bit and make her feel better. And that's it. I can't believe all this has been going on. But I'm not surprised, come to think of it, we've got more gossips here than any one company needs. And what's worse, you apparently believe them.

J.R. apologized to Richard, and suggested that they talk again at some time in the future. Six weeks later, Richard Carlyle gave J. Robert Harper one month's notice that he was quitting to assume the position of vice president in another organization.

TOUGH-MINDED MANAGEMENT
GETS THE JOB DONE

Practical Problem Statements
for Particular Problems

The general rule in stating problems to problem employees, as we have already noted, is to be specific, nonjudgmental, and low-key. While this general rule is valid for virtually every category of problem behavior, specific problem situations may well arise where the problem-solving manager may require a little practical and tough-minded assistance in wording the problem statement to achieve positive results. The following list of suggested problem statements is not intended to be exhaustive, but it is meant to cover some basic, embarrassing, and recurring problem situations.

The Complaining Employee

Suggested Statement: "Joe, I want to talk to you because several different employees have complained to me now about your complaining—if you'll pardon the little joke—and I'd like to talk to you before the situation gets more serious than it is."

Rationale: This statement lets the employee know that his or her complaining behavior is unpleasant to other employees, and is creating a problem, but the careful and judicious use of humor lets the complainer know that the manager is not contemplating

Nice-Guy Lesson #5

**How you say something can be
as important as what you say.**

an immediate nuclear attack. Since complaining behavior is almost always the result of feelings of powerlessness and inadequacy, and is accompanied by chronically high levels of anxiety, the complainer is likely to be very nervous indeed when confronted by a tough-minded manager. Since most of us pretend that we are sympathetic to the complainer's predicament when we are privately annoyed with this unpleasant behavior, the complainer rarely gets honest feedback (in a world filled with avoidance) about the impact of his or her behavior on others. Stating the problem in a somewhat gentle way is the first, and most constructive, step the manager can take in confronting such behavior.

The Tardy Employee

Suggested Statement: "Ann, I noticed that you came in late this morning—it was 8:30 when I saw you come in—and I'd like to talk to you about that. You've been late several times the last two weeks, and that's unusual for you, so I'd like to talk to you about it."

Rationale: Tardiness may be the most common form of problem behavior in the workplace, and so managerial avoidance is also most common when it comes to dealing effectively with it. The suggested statement here is a basic tough-minded problem statement: It draws attention to the problem without prejudice or accusation, and lets the employee know that the manager is alert to the existence of problem behavior and is going to do something about it. Responsibility for doing something about the problem has now been shifted to the employee.

Tardiness is an area where a preventive policy can be highly effective. Consistency, as always, is a magic managerial word here: If the manager deals with *all* cases of tardiness promptly and fairly, the problem will be lessened, if not eliminated entirely. The manager who hopes that tardiness can be permanently eradicated from the workplace is indulging himself in a useless flight of fancy, but it is not wishful thinking to believe that it can be effectively controlled by tough-minded managerial action.

The Employee with Too Much Personal Business

Suggested Statement: "Liz, I noticed that you spent about thirty minutes on the phone yesterday afternoon, talking to your husband, and that was at a time when the monthly report was already overdue. I want to talk to you about this, now, before it becomes a more serious problem."

Rationale: While the amount of time that an employee spends on personal business during working hours will always be something of a gray area, the tough-minded managerial rule that is always appropriate to such situations is that time spent on personal business becomes a problem when it begins to interfere with getting the job done. The nice-guy manager will rationalize inaction when personal business becomes a problem by saying something like, "I don't have the right to interfere." The tough-minded manager will deal with the situation by making a problem statement like the preceding one that focuses on the fact that personal matters are getting in the way of job performance.

The average employee will rapidly take action to curtail personal visits and calls, to name two familiar interruptions, when the problem is drawn to his or her attention. Some employees may simply not be aware that personal business is inappropriate when it is conducted at length at work, and the clear communication of a preventive policy by the employing organization in this area will help management control any potential problems.

The Employee with Poor Grooming or Offensive Personal Habits

Suggested Statement: "George, I know that this is rather personal, and I really hate to bring it up, but I've had two complaints now from customers about the fact that you have strong body odor, and I'd like to talk with you about what can be done."

Rationale: Perhaps nothing is more embarrassing for any

manager in any work environment than having to confront an employee about an indelicate or offensive personal habit, whatever that may be. The essence of being a nice person in middle-class American life is to keep one's body clean and inoffensive, and when this standard is violated in the workplace, it conflicts with another standard of niceness: not mentioning such an indelicate problem.

As always, enough said. If the personal habit is producing complaints from customers, the public, or other employees, then the time has come to take action. As usual, the contemplation of the tough-minded confrontation is much more fearful than the reality. The alternative is clearly *most* unpleasant: having an employee physically present, and close at hand, who offends commonly held standards of conduct and decency.

A case in point occurred some years ago at a large food-processing company headquartered in St. Louis, where a particularly aggressive male employee had for years made sexually oriented suggestions to female employees throughout the company. While numerous employees complained privately about the individual's behavior, it was not until an angry female employee took direct action after hearing such a suggestion (she slapped his face), that the behavior ceased. As is the case with any problem behavior, until its perpetrator was given clear and unmistakable feedback about its inappropriateness, he was convinced that the behavior was O.K. and even welcomed by other employees. Every thoughtful manager is of course grateful for tough-minded employees who solve such problems of personal and interpersonal conduct for them.

MORE TOUGH-MINDED MANAGEMENT
GETS THE JOB DONE

Don't Get Mad
When You Make a Mistake

Making mistakes, in addition to the fear of not being nice, is one of the great phobias of the American middle class. To make a mistake is just about the worst thing in the world that can happen, you might think, if you witness the extraordinary behavior of persons who have committed mistakes. They lie about it; they deny it; they blame the mistake on everyone else; and worse, they work themselves into an emotional turmoil about the situation. You might ask, why is it that making a mistake is so psychologically traumatic to so many people?

Without getting into this subject at great length, since it will distract us from our present purpose (which is precisely to learn how to deal with managerial mistakes that we are *all* going to make), mistakes are often frightening to their authors because they trigger deep-seated feelings of guilt, i.e., a dread fear that we have done something *bad*, and feelings of lack of worth, e.g., "I'm just no good: I screwed up that situation so badly." Many persons are raised, unfortunately, in such guilt-ridden environments and homes. Perfectionistic, insecure parents and teachers punish and humiliate children for their errors, and effectively, if inadvertently, pass on the guilt syndrome from one generation to the next.

In general, the need to cover up or deny mistakes is related to low self-esteem. Several psychologists and philosophers, including Abraham Maslow, have noted that one of the acid tests of maturity is the willingness to *admit* one's errors, and to deal with them in a constructive way. This is no easy task, especially because we all make lots of mistakes—some bright and breathtaking, and some humble and dumb. Some of the most brilliant entrepreneurs in the history of the American nation, including Walt Disney, have achieved their greatest successes after their greatest failures, including the ignominy of going broke after a series of really serious blunders. Making mistakes is something that is second nature to the entrepreneur, including the present author.

The first step in learning to deal with mistakes constructively, and to learn from them, is to admit them, and *not get mad*. Anger is frequently a cover for fear, and when a mistake has been made, the fear that follows is usually a fear that we are somehow incompetent and dumb. A useful mental exercise for a lot of us is to learn to say to ourselves that mistakes are normal and natural, and that we are still good people even though we may have screwed up a bit. A second useful exercise is to become aware that if we get mad after a mistake has been committed, we are normally going to shoot ourselves right in the foot.

Getting mad at either ourselves or others will normally make a mistake, or a problem situation, worse.

A problem-solving manager who is not getting results with a particularly nettlesome employee may well feel such anger, i.e., anger covering fear—a fear that we may *never* be able to deal effectively with this particular problem. If this anger boils over into an ugly confrontation with the employee, a mistake has been made, alas. Such a mistake, however, may lead to a constructive outcome. When a manager gets mad, the employee may be manipulating the situation, but at least he or she knows that the manager *cares* about the problem situation; and that something is likely to be done to rectify it in the future, even if the present situation is something of a mutual shouting match.

When the manager calms down after the confrontation has ended, and regains his tough-minded composure, he or she can always call the employee back in, apologize for getting angry, and resume the problem-solving approach to getting results. Anger *does* motivate both managers and employees to resolve a problem situation, since it is such an unpleasant and energy-draining emotion. In a world filled with stress and pressure, some of these confrontations are bound to ensue in even a normally serene atmosphere; learning to put them to constructive use is yet another facet of the art of tough-minded management—a life-long learning challenge for the student of management and for the managerial practitioner.

Chapter 6

HEA' COME DE JUDGE!
HEA' COME DE JUDGE!

Since the subject of elephants has been introduced, there is a famous poem about six blind men from Industan and an elephant:

> *It was six men of Industan*
> *To learn much inclined,*
> *Who went to see the elephant*
> *Though all of them were blind*
> *That each by observation*
> *Might satisfy his mind.*

The first man falls against the side of the elephant and believes that it's a wall, while the second feels a tusk and thinks that it's a spear. The third grasps the trunk, and concludes that it's a snake; the fourth feels a knee and assumes it's a tree. The fifth finds an ear and thinks that it's a fan, and the sixth seizes the tail and confuses it with a rope.

> *And so these men of Industan*
> *Disputed loud and long,*
> *Each in his opinion*
> *Exceeding stiff and strong;*
> *Though each was partly in the right,*
> *And all were in the wrong.*[1]

Each of us, if we are reasonably normal human beings, has a little man in our head who runs most of our thought processes.

This little man, in the words of Flip Wilson of "Laugh-In" fame, is "de judge." He performs an important survival function for us, but he is also responsible for many of the hilarious and erroneous mistakes we make. He is a busy, busy, busy little person, and he is never so occupied as when he is making judgments about other people.

In a light-hearted way, an important topic has been introduced that is vitally important to effectively solving problem-employee situations: learning *not* to judge the employee, or at least to suspend judgment for as long as humanly possible in the search for a solution. Perhaps firstly, though, we should briefly examine why judgmental thinking is so basic in our repertoire of cognitive functions.

What Judging Is and Why We Do It

Judgments are evaluative statements—that is, they are statements of good versus bad, right versus wrong, black versus white. They do not so much describe what is going on in the world as what is going on in us. For example, two sports enthusiasts arise bright and early, look out through their bedroom windows, and see that it is snowing heavily. The first, a jogger, mutters, "What a rotten day." The second, a skier, begins whistling, "Oh What a Beautiful Morning."

After a tardy employee has come in late again this morning, and the manager has done nothing yet again, the manager scowls and says, "That Sally is a lazy no-good bum." The judgment that has just been made about Sally, as were the earlier statements, is really just what psychologists call a *projection* of the manager's feelings. At bottom, the manager feels badly about himself because he or she hasn't done anything to change Sally's behavior, and the problem is snowballing (no pun intended).

Estimates vary, but probably half to two-thirds of all our thoughts and statements have some degree of judgmentalism in them.[2] Why are judgments so common, you might ask? The reason has to do with the evolution of the species and particularly with regard to what pre-historic man had to do to survive in a danger-filled world. When that early man looked out of his cave one foggy morning and saw a large animal flashing by, he had to make a quick decision: Friend or foe? Should I flee or should I fight? Am I his food or is he mine? Roughly the same judgment had to be made whenever a strange human was encountered.

It is a tribute to the accuracy of man's judgments that the species has flourished. Nonetheless, the process has some sharp limitations. When we meet a stranger at a casual social gathering in a genteel suburb, we make an almost instantaneous fight-or-flight, like-dislike judgment about that person. This judgment is called a first impression, and it may be either strikingly perceptive or just plain wrong. The stranger smiles warmly: We like. The stranger frowns and looks away, preoccupied with financial problems encountered earlier in the day, and we judge him as dangerously hostile: We dislike. First impressions have incredible endurance and stubbornly resist change. We are condemned by the very ability that saved mankind.

While these short paragraphs represent yet another fast tour of a very large territory, they do illustrate how powerful a very basic habit of mind is. Not only is judgmentalism powerful, it is very hard to put it on hold. As we shall see, however, the ability to suspend judgment is a necessary skill for the manager in effectively coping with problem situations.

How to Give Employees a Fair Hearing

Our ardent auditor, Mr. Loveless, returns to the scene. He has just heard his manager complete his statement of the problem with, "Could you tell me what happened or what you remember about that?" After a brief pause, after some squirming, and after much apparent reflection, the following reply is forthcoming:

> Gee, Mary said I pinched her? At the water cooler? Well, gosh, I remember walking down the aisle next to the cooler, yeah, that would've been around three o'clock, but I sure didn't pinch her or anything. She said I pinched her?

The manager's response is, "Yes, she said you pinched her." After another brief pause for thought, Mr. Loveless continues:

Well, I sure didn't pinch her, but come to think of it, that aisle next to the water cooler is real narrow, there are those big filing cabinets on either side of the aisle, and I remember I was carrying this big stack of binders on the Quality Auto-maker Co. audit. Gosh, it was such a big stack I could hardly see around them. And those binders have sharp edges. Anyway, I saw Mary there by the water cooler, and I said, "Excuse me," when I went by, and she kind of ran away and sort of looked upset. I wonder if I bumped against her with those binders as I passed by?

The manager asks, "Are you saying you think you might have hit her with the binders?" Mr. Loveless replies:

Yeah, geez, that has to be it. Now I know why she looked upset. She thought I'd pinched her. Those metal corners must have hit her as I was going by, 'cause I couldn't see real well where I was going.

The little bitty judge in the manager's head has now leaped to his feet and is screaming loudly, "He's a damned liar. He's making it up. Even if he was carrying the binders, he obviously reached under and sneaked in a pinch. He's been pulling this for years, and he's not getting away with it this time." The gavel slams down, and the case is closed: Defendant guilty as charged.

The point here, of course, is that it is very hard indeed to silence the judgmental aspects of thought. To this point in the interview, the manager has actually done an admirable job of not getting sucked into *agreement* or *disagreement* with the employee's statement, whatever may be going on in the privacy of his head. All he has done, after hearing Loveless state that he thinks he might have hit Mary Reilly accidentally with the binders, is to ask a *clarifying* question that presupposes neither innocence nor guilt, but simply seeks to clarify what the employee has said.

Such a question, although it is phrased in interrogatory fashion, is really a restatement of what the employee has said. "You think you might have hit her with the binders?" is a completely nonjudgmental inquiry because it seeks only clarification and/or additional information. It tells the employee that the manager is interested in what happened and wants to listen to the employee, but it doesn't seek to evaluate the statement. It is one of the basic counseling and interviewing skills that an effective problem-solving manager must learn to use and that are employed extensively in giving the employee a fair hearing.

For in this phase of the interview, and in any early problem-solving intervention, the manager's goal is *not* to determine who was guilty and who was innocent, but who did what to whom. In a benevolent way, he doesn't even care about guilt or innocence. What he is concerned with is dealing with the problem situation so that it does not recur; so that if Lowell Loveless really did bump into Mary Reilly accidentally, he'll explain that to her and make sure that it doesn't happen again. And, so that if Mary made up the whole incident because she's mad at Lowell for bawling her out unfairly, she won't do that again.

This is not to say that the manager does not care about sexual harassment in his office. Of course he does, but he communicates that concern without saying it explicitly in his statement of the problem. As we noted earlier, by including the pinching complaint in his problem statement, the manager was telling the employee that this is unacceptable behavior, if it occurred, but he's communicating without moralizing or pontificating. When the employee hears the manager say, " . . . and you know, we can't have that kind of behavior in this organization," he is simply offended, for all the reasons mentioned previously.

Realistically, in many situations like the one we have been analyzing, the manager will *never* know what actually happened. He is dealing with one employee's word against another's, with each employee's eyewitness account of the incident subject to all of the inaccuracies and distortions that eyewitness accounts are famous for. Any time the manager spends in conducting a criminal investigation will be time wasted. The manager's most effective role in this phase of the interview is really quite a simple one: To *listen* to the employee sympathetically, but nonjudgmentally, and to clarify the employee's role in the problem with a view to getting action out of the employee that will solve it. This role is relatively easy for the manager to play, providing that he understands why he needs to do it and what the payoff is going to be for him. The skills involved are quite easy to learn.

When the manager listens to the employee and asks a few clarifying questions along the way, an interesting psychological process begins to unfold in the employee. Responsibility has been transferred to him or her and the process has become what the therapist Carl Rogers called "client centered."[3] Firstly, he begins thinking about the problem, either with a view to clarifying his role in what happened or to constructing a web of lies that will cover his backside satisfactorily. Whether clarifying or lying, however, he is also busy doing a second thing; namely, figuring out what he can do to extricate himself from his predicament and solve the problem. As we have already noted, he will be powerfully motivated to solve the problem. No employee wants to sit in front of his friendly manager, explaining what actually happened in the aisle next to the water cooler.

The use of good listening skills of course encourages the employee to talk, and that in itself is an important problem-solving mechanism. The more the employee talks, the better he will feel. The more he talks, the more he will perceive the manager as friendly. The more he talks, the more he will think of ways the problem can be solved, so he can get out of the manager's office and get back to work.

Listening is such an easy and effective skill to use, it is always a little surprising to a casual observer that it isn't used more frequently. The reason is that while listening itself is relatively easy to do, getting out of the judge's role is more difficult. Judges don't listen, they hand out verdicts. Once the manager is convinced that giving the employee a hearing and spending most of the time in that hearing listening to the person is a good use of his time, then it is much more likely that he will do precisely that.

Some Further Notes on Clarifying Skills

Clarifying skills have a common theme, even though they vary a bit in expression. They always involve some degree of repetition of what the employee has said, and this repetition is often expressed in the form of a question. As we have already noted, clarification is not evaluation. The manager can give the employee a sympathetic hearing and win the cooperation of the employee, without ever once agreeing or disagreeing with his statements.

One of the games employees like to play, in fact, is sucking the supervisor into agreeing with their account of events or trapping the manager into arguing with them. Either way, the manager loses. If the manager says to the ever-present Mr. Loveless, "Well, Lowell, I can sure see what you're saying. It must have been an accident, and Mary just misunderstood," avoidance has triumphed again. And if he says, as did his judge in an earlier passage, "Lowell, how can you expect me to believe that?," the stage has been set for a fight.

One clarifying skill that will help conclude the hearing of the problem, once the employee has had an adequate opportunity to give his account (not version) of what happened, is *summarization*. The summary is just that: normally, a one-sentence wrap-up of the entire situation. In our ongoing example, the manager can summarize succinctly by saying something like, "So your understanding is that it was an accident, and Mary didn't realize it?" Even though the summary statement is nonjudgmental, it has a wonderful connotation embodied in it: It suggests that some action should be taken. If there was a misunderstanding, for example, then that should be cleared up.

Two other skills that are widely used by counselors and therapists, but that are not mysterious at all, are *repetition* and *paraphrasing*. Both these skills are particularly useful in coaxing a recalcitrant employee into talking more freely, and they are normally used most effectively at a time when the employee has stopped talking completely or has apparently paused for thought. If Mr. Loveless, again, has paused after saying, "I may have bumped against her with the binders," the manager can simply say, "You may have bumped against her?" While repetition sounds somewhat simple-minded, and it is, to the employee it conveys the message that the manager is interested and wants to hear more, so it is normally not an awkward or intrusive device in the employee's mind.

Paraphrasing is close to repetition, although it involves some restatement of what the employee has been saying. The restatement, or rephrasing, is usually done to clear up something that might not be understood by both parties. If we may use Mr. Loveless yet again:

Lowell: I was carrying a big stack of binders, and I could

	barely see where I was going in that narrow aisle next to the water cooler, and I think I kind of tripped or lurched or something as I got near the cooler.
Manager:	So you think you may have stumbled a bit as you approached the cooler?
Lowell:	Yeah, that's what must have happened. I must have stumbled right into her with those binders as I got near the cooler.

Like repetition, the skill is nonjudgmental and does not add to or interpret anything the employee has said.

In the case of any employee who is very withdrawn and is having difficulty speaking, another skill that can be used effectively by the manager is the *direct factual* question. This skill is a little more tricky than the other clarifying skills we've discussed because factual questions can easily become accusatory, and the interview can degenerate into an interrogation. Nonetheless, if the employee is not responding to the manager's handling of the problem, something must normally be attempted to draw him out of his shell, or a constructive outcome will be difficult.

If Mr. Loveless has remained silent after hearing the manager's statement of the problem, after a moment or two, the manager might follow-up with something like, "I wonder if you could just take a minute or two, Lowell, to think about what you were doing yesterday afternoon. Do you recall your movements between two and four, say?" In this example, the manager is telling the employee that it is all right for him to take his time and gather his thoughts before speaking.

Since judgmentalism is so powerful and basic, however, it is all too easy for the manager to slip into something like, "Now, Lowell, were you or were you *not* near the water cooler at three?" Once this process begins, the employee is likely to be even more defensive and silent. Because the manager needs some sort of response from the employee, an option that is always open to him and that does not constitute avoidance, is to say something like the following to a silent employee, "I can understand if you might need some time to think more about this and that's O.K. with me. Why don't you come back this afternoon, and we'll talk about it again."

The Long-Term Goal of Tough-Minded Problem Solving

It's the long-term goal of every tough-minded problem-solving manager to create an organizational environment where most problems solve themselves. In this world, seldom achieved on this earth, the employee comes forward spontaneously, defines the problem, clarifies it, solves it and leaves. The manager sits benignly on his or her chair, smokes a pipe, and concludes by saying, "That's very good, Joe."

Everyone can dream, of course. In the real world, however, something similar *does* happen when an excellent employee, for example, who genuinely likes and respects his manager, unexpectedly has his car break down on the freeway and arrives for work 35 minutes late. This person does not dither around. He marches promptly into the manager's office where the following exchange occurs:

Employee: George, I'm awfully sorry I was more than a half hour late this morning. You probably saw me coming in just now. That damned old clunker of mine, you know that '79 Chevy I've been using as a second car, threw the transmission on I-84 this morning. Parts all over the highway. What a mess.

Manager: I'm sorry to hear that, Joe.

Employee: Well, anyway, that's it for the Chevy. I can't be coming in for work late, so I'm trading it in on a little Subaru *tonight*. Those little Subarus never break down, and the Chevy's been giving me fits. So, tomorrow I ought to be here with transmission intact. By the way, George, that technical report on our new minicomputer is due in Portland tomorrow morning, and since I lost a little time this morning, I'm going to stay late tonight to finish it up. It'll be waiting on your desk tomorrow morning.

Manager: Thanks for offering to finish it up today, Joe. I sure hope you have better luck with the new car.

It is the experience of every effective manager that in a well-run organization, high performance employees do this all the time. When a problem occurs, they solve it. If a problem recurs, they become even more ingenious so that it can be taken care of permanently. Most managers would kill to have an office made up entirely of such people.

This is exactly what happens when a manager has a reputation for being effective. Good people seek him or her out and work productively and hard under his management. Good management inspires confidence, breeds creativity, and leads to high productivity over the long haul. Most organizations that have one eye and half a brain, in the words of an old Canadian hockey joke, would kill to keep the manager.

The real tragedy of nice-guy management is that it not only produces chaos in the short to medium run, it creates an environment where the tough-guy approach is *necessary* in the short run just to restore a semblance of order in the organization. When the history of such a company is written, after its eventual bankruptcy, the historians must chronicle a series of flip-flops from nice-guy to tough-guy management, and back. The tough-guy manager, after he has alienated everyone in the organization and fear has run its course, is frequently replaced by a nice guy who now falls all over himself being considerate to formerly abused employees.

Woe is due the organization that does not solve its problems intelligently, immediately, and permanently. We have finally begun to recognize the truth of this proposition in American management, and the organizational histories that are written 50 years from now will begin to reflect that recognition.

STEP 3:
GIVING THE EMPLOYEE A FAIR HEARING AND CLARIFYING THE PROBLEM

- Tell the little man in your head, your judge, to be *quiet.* Keep your private opinion of the employee's guilt or innocence private.

- Spend most of your time *listening* to the employee.

- Use nonjudgmental skills, such as *repetition, paraphrasing,* and *summarization* to help clarify what the employee is saying.

- Ask *direct factual* questions if the employee is unresponsive.

- Do not get sucked into *agreeing* or *disagreeing* with the employee. If an argument develops, reschedule the interview.

A CONSTRUCTIVE DIALOGUE

Let's stop for a minute and look at some of these tough-minded management techniques in practice. Observe how the professor in the following dialogue uses some of the techniques just described to help a student work through and resolve a problem.

"The College of Computer Science"

Jim Winters was 25, a high school graduate, and had recently returned to college after serving six years in the United States Marine Corps. After talking with a career counselor, he chose to enroll in the College of Computer Science because his high school mathematics grades had been good, he was interested in computers, and he believed that career prospects in the computer field were excellent. He had not had any previous experience with computers, however, or with the field of data processing.

After he had been in his introductory computer science class for three weeks, he approached the instructor, Dr. Richard Nyland, and explained that he was considering dropping the class:

Winters: Dr. Nyland, I really like you, and the class has been very interesting, but I think I'm going to have to drop the course. I don't think my aptitude for computer science is as good as I thought it was, and I'm afraid I'm going to flunk the course.

Nyland: I'm really surprised and sorry to hear you say that, Jim. You got a passing grade on your first quiz, didn't you?

Winters: Yeah, you gave me a "B," but I think it was just a fluke. The other students in the class know so much more about computers than I do, it almost makes me sick.

Nyland: They're more knowledgeable than you?

Winters: Gosh, are they ever. They're such smart kids, and they know everything about bytes, data bases, RAM, and floppy disks. Half the time I don't even know what they're talking about, and I feel like such a dummy. I just know I'm in way over my head in this course, and so I think I'll just ask you for permission to drop right now.

Nyland: Before you drop the course, Jim, do you think you're expected to know everything about data bases and the other things you mentioned after you finish this course?

Winters: Well, in your syllabus you stressed that this was just an introductory course.

Nyland: Yes I did, and that's what it is, and so far you're doing fine. Did you realize that most of the kids in the class have been taking computer courses of one kind or another since junior high school?

Winters: No, gee, I didn't realize that. It's no wonder, then, that they know so many computer terms. And I'm so much older than most of them that I kind of feel like a fish out of water anyway. Come to think of it, a lot of the stuff they're talking about when we have the class breaks isn't going to be covered in this course anyway, according to your syllabus, and I'll be taking it later on. I guess I just feel intimidated by all the terms these kids know, and how smart they seem.

Nyland: That's probably just what it is, Jim, because you're doing fine in the class so far.

Winters: You know, I did get a "B" in the quiz, and I've understood everything we've been talking about so far. I think I'll just hang in there in the course, now that we've talked. You know, you're such a fine instructor that I think I might take more of my computer classes with you.

ENDNOTES

1. From the well-known parable by John G. Saxe.

2. See Murial Schiffman, *Gestalt Self Therapy and Further Techniques for Personal Growth* (Menlo Park, CA: Self-Therapy Press, 1972) for an analysis of the roots of the phenomenon of judgmentalism.

3. Carl Rogers, *Client-Centered Therapy: Its Current Practice, Implications and Theory* (Boston: Houghton-Mifflin Company, 1951).

TOUGH-MINDED MANAGEMENT GETS THE JOB DONE

Coping with Massive Managerial Overreaction and Hysteria

A special category of problem behavior, often encountered by the author in his years in the worlds of academia, industry, and government, is the manager who overreacts wildly, and almost hysterically, to any and all problem situations. While this behavior is obviously rooted in insecurity, and is frequently amusing to outside observers, it is not at *all* funny to the person who must cope with the frenzied behavior of managers who exhibit what might be called the Chicken Little Syndrome: Every problem, however trivial, is the end of the world, and justifies dramatic and often prejudicial action.

A case in point, drawn from the nervous world of academic administration, demonstrates how self-defeating such behavior can be, and how the chicken-little manager brings about the very things he or she fears, as does any determined neurotic. A woman inherited the directorship of an evening-division program at a distinguished small private liberal arts college in Philadelphia from a hapless predecessor who had nearly bankrupted the program through poor financial management. When the woman took over the program, she was very concerned about the quality of instruction in the business courses, because this had been another weakness of the program in the previous administration.

When a new instructor, whom we shall call Prima Donald, was hired to teach management courses at the college, the director asked him if he would be interested in teaching in the evening division. He replied that he would, and soon was teaching small-business management on Wednesday evenings in a Philadelphia suburb. After the second class meeting, he got a call from the

Nice-Guy Lesson #6

**Tough-minded management begins
with NOT making snap judgments.**

director, who in a worried (almost frantic) tone of voice told him that she was "very, very concerned" about the problems he was having with the small-business management course. Since he felt that the course had been going very well, he asked her in tones of surprise what problems she was talking about. She then told him that one of the students in the course had complained about a "serious lack of content" in Prima's teaching, and that she was very concerned that he beef up the course content in future sessions.

He then asked her if the student had called her to complain about him. "Oh no," she replied, "I had just called one or two of them to see how the class was going, and this one student remarked that there was a lack of content." Prima held his temper, somewhat uncharacteristically, and asked her if she would reveal the name of the student. Somewhat reluctantly, she did. At the next class session, during a coffee break, Donald pulled the student aside, and asked, "Joe, did you tell the director that there's a serious lack of content in my course? It looks to me like you've been enjoying the course."

The student quickly replied, "Oh no, Dr. Donald, is that what she said? I didn't say that at all."

Donald: Well, what did you say then, Joe? Can you tell me what happened? The director tells me that she called you up, "just to see how the course was going." Did she do that?

Joe: Is that what she said? Well, what happened is that she called me all right, but what she said, in this real worried voice is, "Joe, is everything going all right in Prima Donald's course? Could you tell me if everything's all right?" Well when I heard her talking like that, I immediately assumed there had been some major problem, like you had gone nuts and raped one of the women in class or something, so I got real nervous myself, thinking I might have to be a witness or something. Dr. Donald, I really like your class, but since she seemed to be fishing for something real negative about you, I thought maybe I should say something a little critical. I sure didn't have any guts, did I? So what I said was that you teach the class in a seminar format, since we're all adult students, and that if you used this same format—with the informal discussions and cases, instead of relying exclusively on the textbook and lectures—that some of the young kids in the daytime classes on the campus might not like this format. Now I like it fine, of course, and so do most of the others in the class. And that's all I said, sir, honest. I just wish now that I had kept my big mouth shut. She always calls us, you know, about every instructor. I hate it.

Donald: Don't be mad at yourself, Joe, I'm going to have a little talk with her.

Joe: Well, I hope you won't be too hard on her, Dr. Donald. She's nice, you know, and she really cares about the program, but we all call her "the twitch" because she's so nervous. She'll just drive you crazy when she calls you up on the phone.

Two days later, Prima met with the director in her office, and in a calm and measured voice made the following points: (1) By calling students in a nervous voice to ask how things were going in a course, she was inadvertently encouraging student complaints; (2) students felt that such calls were unprofessional and demeaning to faculty members teaching in the program; and (3) the information she was receiving as a result of the phone calls was biased and misleading, and was magnifying any problems that might exist in the program.

The director listened thoughtfully to his comments, apologized for making the calls, and assured Prima that such calls would not be made in the future. Two months later, during a class break in a personnel management course that he was teaching for the evening division, a student approached Dr. Donald and asked him if he had been having problems with the course. "I got a call yesterday from the assistant director of the program," she said, "and he just wanted to know if there were any problems in the course that he should know about."

As the preceding vignette illustrates all too clearly, there is no easy way to deal with the manager who is chronically anxious. These people often succeed, unfortunately, in transmitting their fears and worries to others around them, and they often create problems, which keeps their self-defeating fears alive. In the long run, they usually succeed in creating the thing they fear (which often means losing their jobs), but in the short run they often make life hell for their subordinates and colleagues. The fact that the chaos they create is inadvertent is small comfort for the person forced to work in a neurotically anxious environment.

There is often no easy way to deal with managerial hysteria, but the author is reminded of the timeless cliché about keeping one's head while all about are losing theirs. Remaining calm around a neurotically anxious person is a major step toward winning the battle, although this can be difficult. A second step, as was illustrated in the preceding case, is firmly and tough-mindedly reminding them that the problem, whatever it is, *can be solved*, and is not the end of the world. A third step, which does have Machiavellian overtones (although it is rooted in the need to be sane and to survive), is to draw to their attention the fact that they have magnified or created the problem.

In the author's experience, avoidance strategies are frequently engaged in by employees and fellow managers when they are confronted with a neurotic manager (the faithful reader will not faint with pure surprise, we can safely assume), and the most commonly used of these strategies is gossiping and complaining about the neurotic manager's behavior. While the uselessness of complaining as a means of changing behavior has been remarked upon by many wise authors, the fact that this behavior continues to be universal is a tribute to the enduring power of avoidance, as well as to the fact that in the short run complaining brings some satisfaction to the complainer. In the long run, however, the complainer alienates all about him, and must still deal with the problem that he complains about.

Chapter 7

GETTING A PROMISE
OF ACTION OR CHANGE
THAT WILL SOLVE THE PROBLEM

In early December of 1987, David Burke, aged 35, boarded Pacific Southwest Airlines Flight 1771 from Los Angeles to San Francisco. Because he was a former employee of the airline, he was familiar to security personnel and thus was able to bypass normal security-screening procedures. Halfway to its destination, Flight 1771 sent out a distress call indicating that there was gunfire on board and the flight was going down. Two minutes later, the commuter jet slammed into the ground, killing all 43 persons aboard, including David Burke and his former manager at PSA, Raymond Thomson.

An investigation revealed that less than a month before, Thomson had fired Burke for stealing $69 in cocktail receipts. Burke borrowed a .44 magnum revolver and carried it aboard Flight 1771. Investigators found one of his thumb prints on the revolver when it was retrieved from the wreckage of the flight, along with a threatening note that he had written to Thomson. Burke apparently shot both the pilot and copilot, precipitating the crash that killed all aboard.[1]

The short case that introduced this chapter is a violent tragedy of the sort that has been reported at least once in every American state in this decade. It is unique neither to the public nor to the private sectors. It can happen anywhere and almost anytime. It is not perhaps so unfortunate that these episodes are unnecessary as that they can usually and easily be prevented by good management. The problem-solving manager uses interview-closing skills that resolve most problems well short of termination, but when a firing is required, it is done with dignity and gentleness.

Techniques for Closing the Interview: Getting a Promise of Action

Our friend, Mr. Loveless, has returned to the scene. He has just explained that he thinks he must have hit Mary Reilly with the binders as he was going by. We pick up the dialogue at this point:

Manager: So you couldn't see very well?

Lowell: No, those binders are so darned heavy, and I was really struggling with them, but out of the corner of my eye I saw her sort of rush down the aisle, the other way, as I was saying. I thought she looked upset, but I haven't seen her since.

Manager: So you haven't had a chance to talk to her?

Lowell: No, I haven't, but I'm going to go down and talk to her as soon as I leave here. This is all a misunderstanding, but I don't want her thinking I goosed her by the water fountain for God's sake. I'm married, with three kids, and I can't have people thinking I pinched her. So I'm going to tell her what happened, just like I'm telling you now, and I'm going to tell her I'm sorry, and that it won't happen again. I'm sure that'll help clear things up.

Manager: Well, thanks, Lowell. I'm sure that will be helpful. You say you're going to do that today?

Lowell: Yeah, you'd better believe it. I want this cleared up. I'm going to do it right away.

At this point, the odds are long that the problem has been solved. Loveless has volunteered to take action to resolve the dispute, and if he follows up on what he has told the manager, the odds are that Mary will accept his explanation (whether she believes it or not), and there will no further occurrences of pinching or accidental bumping. The problem-solving goal has been achieved, short of a formal action of any sort.

In this interview, the manager knew exactly what he wanted. He wanted Lowell to *volunteer* to take action to clear things up, and Lowell was obliging enough to do just that. One is reminded of the ancient adage about taking the horse to water. In this case, the employee was highly motivated to do something, partly because he saw all kinds of trouble looming and was bright enough to seize the initiative. The manager was prepared, however, to move to the next step for getting action to solve the problem if Lowell did not; namely, *suggesting* an action the employee could take to solve the problem.

Often the employee will be so nonplussed by the interview situation that he will be unable to think of an action he might take, or he will just not realize that he is in a position to do something. If the manager sees that the employee is in a bit of a muddle, but apparently not highly defensive and resisting action, he might just say something like, "Lowell, you mentioned that you haven't had a chance to talk to Mary since yesterday. Could I suggest that you stop by and talk with her sometime today, just to clear things up?" Hopefully, the response will be, "Oh yeah, that would be good. I just hadn't thought of that. I'll do it this afternoon."

In both of these examples, the assumption has been that this is the first interview dealing with the problem and that the employee has demonstrated a basic willingness to cooperate with the supervisor. This assumption is usually sound if the manager has intervened early, before hostilities have built up, and before the employee has developed a sense that his behavior is O.K. The manager is thus in a position to make very gentle use of his authority and in essence give the employee a "nudge" toward taking action.

If the problem continues, however, or if the employee resists action or begins playing games (much more on this shortly), then the manager must begin to make more use of authority. This does not imply a flip-flop to tough-guy techniques, however, just judicious use of authority. In our familiar example, if Loveless said something like, "Oh, I'd feel kind of embarrassed about talking to her," after hearing the manager suggest that he do that, the manager can respond with a statement that is both supportive and directive. "Lowell, I can understand that you might feel that way, but I really think it would help clear this up if you'd talk to

Mary today. So I'm going to *ask* you to do that." The manager is still acting as a friend, but the nudge has become a tug, even though the chances for an informal resolution still seem good.

In situations where there is an underlying problem that might eventually require outside professional help, it may not be possible to resolve the situation without exercising still more authority. Even when this is necessary, it can still be done without resorting to tough-guy tactics, and without the manager once stepping out of his role as problem solver and friend. If we may introduce a plot twist in our saga of the auditor:

Lowell: Well, I'm not really sure I want to talk to Mary because the more I think about this, the more I'm sure she knows I didn't pinch her, and that if there was any contact at all, it was from the binders. I think she's mad at me about something, and she's kind of trumping this up to get back at me.

Manager: Well, Lowell, I can't be the judge of that, and I guess there's no way I can ever really know what happened, but I'd like to get this cleared up so I'm just going to *tell* you that I want you to talk to Mary. So, before you leave, would you promise me that you'll do that, just so we can get this settled?

Lowell: Well, okay, I'll talk to her if you really want, but I sure didn't pinch her.

Manager: Thanks for saying you'll talk to her. I think that'll help clear things up.

The manager is being ever more firm, but is still very much a problem solver and is still being careful to be nonjudgmental. He has neither agreed nor disagreed with Lowell's assertion that Mary is "trumping this up," but has continued to focus on the goal of getting things settled now.

In some cases, for a host of reasons, an informal solution is just not going to be possible, and formal disciplinary machinery is going to come into action. Even when letters of reprimand, suspensions, loss of pay, and termination may be required, the manager still does not have to be punitive. His role does change, however, for he now becomes the person who is the principle source of feedback for the employee about what will happen if action that will resolve matters is not taken. It becomes the manager's responsibility to *spell out the consequences* of not taking action. This can perhaps best be illustrated, again, in the form of dialogue:

Manager: Fred, we've discussed your tardiness twice now, and you've promised me that your performance would improve. I'm sorry to have to say that you've been late twice again this week and that if you're late one more time, you're going to leave me no choice but to write a formal letter of reprimand about this that will stay in your personnel file for six months. Do you understand what I'm saying?

Fred: Yeah, but believe me, you won't have to write that letter because I'm going to sell that damned old car now. This is ridiculous. I just have to get better transportation.

Manager: I sure hope you'll do that because I really don't want to have to write that letter.

In this instance, the manager has made it very clear what will happen if there is even one more late arrival, but he has also reiterated an important problem-solving concept. It is the employee's responsibility to do something to rectify the situation. This point has been made without moralizing or pontificating; the manager has only said, "You're going to leave me no choice but to . . . ."

In cases where more than one interview is required, the manager will usually begin with a modified problem statement that includes a brief factual review of actions and promises, but still continues to avoid accusations and recriminations. Listening to the employee still occurs, but this phase of the interview tends to become shorter, unless new or unexpected developments have occurred. The employee has heard what the consequences will be if his or her performance does not improve, and the whole interaction will have a somewhat more somber tone.

The Art of the Gentle and Dignified Firing

Most supervisors simply hate, and fear, having to fire an employee. That is why there is so much avoidance about it, and why firings are so poorly and traumatically handled. Every tragic tale of a dismissed employee returning to murder his or her former boss undoubtedly leads to even more avoidance of the issue.

Most firings in the real world take place at four o'clock on Friday afternoon. The employee is told that he's fired, is given his final paycheck, is told to clean out his desk, and when he leaves, the locks are changed. The symbolic changing of the locks is a tacit admission that the firing is an angry and punitive act, and that the organization must be protected in the future against possible retaliation by the employee. Some firings are handed over to the personnel department for "disposition."

It is not surprising that employees often react with anger to such treatment. For one thing, when they are fired on Friday, their entire weekend has simply been ruined because they will have no real opportunity to begin work on seeking employment elsewhere. If word gets back to them that locks have been changed, they realistically view that as antagonistic and as a sign they can't be trusted. The firing becomes far more traumatic than it needs to be.

This is not to suggest that terminations are ever pleasant, and employees will often use the firing to lay massive guilt trips on supervisors. A steel foreman who had just fired an alcohol- and drug-dependent employee, who had literally fallen down several times near molten steel, was treated to the following heart-rending statements:

> You son of a bitch! You're signing my death warrant. I've lost my family, my friends, and now you're taking away my job. I've got nothing left. What am I going to do now? You're just condemning me to death.

The foreman was a very shaken individual indeed, and when quizzed by the author, he blurted out that he felt terrible because he had fired an employee. After being reassured that he had done the right thing (in this case, the employee posed a real and immediate danger to himself and his coworkers) and that he hadn't signed anyone's "death warrant," he promised that he would follow up on the case. The doomed worker soon joined the local chapter of Alcoholics Anonymous, quit drinking and abusing drugs, was reunited with his family within three months and regained his job in a year. The firing was a real favor to the worker. It let him know changes had to be made, and they were, but not without pain.

Unfortunately, the firing is often the bitter medicine the employee needs to get well, particularly where drugs and alcohol are involved. Since alcohol- and drug-dependent employees are often extremely bright, it is precisely these employees who are extremely adept at concealing the problem for a long time and skillfully manipulating the manager, often using guilt, when he or she attempts to intervene. A short note on the case of the steel worker: He was fired, not because he had been drinking, but because he posed a danger to himself and others. His performance was unsatisfactory.

Poor performance is always the reason for firing. Even if the supervisor suspects that an employee is having problems with drugs or alcohol, he does not have a right to intervene until the employee's performance becomes a problem. When the performance does become a problem, then he has both a right and a duty to take action, and the termination of the employee is his sad, final duty when all other actions have failed. Effective firings can be both gentle and dignified:

Manager: Fred, I'm terribly sorry that it's come to this, but your extreme tardiness has just left me no choice but to terminate you. I'm particularly sad because in the past you were a good employee, and just about everyone here liked you. You can pick up your check at Personnel. Despite this, I want to wish you well at a future job.

The firing is not an act of anger, it is one of sadness. It is a last resort, and it has occurred because the employee has not taken action to improve his performance. Hopefully, it has not occurred because of the *inaction* of the manager and the employee's organization. Gentle and dignified firings are not always possible (let's be realistic), but they are more likely to be achieved if the manager follows a few tough-minded rules.

1. Don't rehash the case at length. If intermediate steps have been taken, the employee knows exactly why he or she is there.
2. Get right to it, but be calm and matter of fact. Treat the employee as an adult, and be courteous.
3. Explain briefly that the employee is being terminated because his performance has been unsatisfactory.
4. If you are sorry that it's come to this, say so. If the employee was once a good employee, say so. But don't get into hypocritical lying.
5. Make sure the employee knows the firing is final. Hand him the letter of termination at the time of the firing. Don't mail it to his home. Let him know where he can pick up his final check or hand it to him.
6. Fire the employee early in the day or early in the week. The four-o'clock-Friday firing is not humane.
7. Before you tell the employee that he is being fired, remind yourself that you may actually be doing him a favor down the road, and spare yourself the guilt trip.
8. *Never* renege on the firing, even if the employee weeps in your office. You can be considerate and hand the employee tissues, but you are being a fool if you renege.

While a firing is never easy, it is less likely to be difficult and angry if the employee is aware that he or she is likely to be terminated. Chickenshit management regularly produces unnecessary trauma at the time of termination for everyone involved. If the firing is to be final, however, the manager had better follow an orderly series of disciplinary steps and have offered to help the employee before the actual termination.

A couple of final notes on firing for the manager who is truly guilt-ridden and hard to convince that he has not done a bad thing by terminating the employee. Firstly, many employees arrange to get themselves fired. They may not always be conscious of their motives, and the process may not be deliberate, but firing is what they bring about, and the process is not always neurotic. The most common underlying theme in the motivated firing is hatred for the job, which manifests itself in a variety of ways (nonattendance, lack of concentration, destructive behavior, boredom, or physical avoidance) that lead to unsatisfactory performance. An ancient Oriental concept that we have already referred to also applies here, saving face. When the employee finally accomplishes termination, he can go home to his wife and say, "See honey, I told you how much they hate me and abuse me down at the shop. Well, now they've fired me." This heroic posture is much more dignified than having to say, "I got so fed up with handling freight for them, I quit."

Secondly, as was the case with the fired steel worker, the firing turns out to be for the best. Charles Swartout, the president of an outplacement firm, has a marvelously instructive (and true) story in this regard:

> I inherited a client who was a senior executive with a large chemical firm. He had been fired a few days earlier, and right after they did it, at four o'clock on Friday, of course, he crawled home abjectly to tell his wife that he had just been terminated. Her reaction was to fling her arms around him and say, "Honey, I'm so glad. You've hated that job for years and years. Now you can find something you really like." Shortly thereafter, we placed him out of state, in a job he liked much, much better, and where he was making about fifteen thousand more a year. He called me up after he had been on the new job a few weeks and said, "Charley, I'm so glad I got fired by the XYZ Company because I'm so much happier at what I'm doing here."[2]

While it would be untrue to suggest that employees look forward to being fired, it is the *fear* of being fired that is much more painful than the actual firing. While a firing always produces fairly major changes in a person's life circumstances, often including relocation and a new type of employer and job, this whole process of change is often energizing and rejuvenating for the person. Once the employee knows that he or she is going to be terminated and deals with the immediate pain and anger, he can busy himself preparing for a new job or career. If one looks at a termination as a chance for the fired employee to begin a whole new and better life, some of the managerial guilt typically surrounding the act will be eased.

A Sequence of Disciplinary Steps and an Offer to Help

It is always the goal of a problem-solving manager to resolve problems informally, short of formal disciplinary action. When formal action does become necessary, however, a few words to the wise. The manager should *always* follow the sequence of steps specified in the union contract or in the personnel handbook. Failure to do so will, at the very least, give the employee grounds to appeal an action and will usually result in the reversal of an adverse action.

In both the public and private sectors, the employee should or must be offered assistance to deal with a problem before being terminated. While there are sound humanitarian reasons for wanting to do this, the problem-solving manager views this as a natural role. In the case of the tardy employee, the offer to help might take the following form:

Manager: Fred, I know you've been telling me that you're having transportation problems, but this is the third time we've talked about it. Is there something else that's been bothering you or that you're having trouble with that I might be able to help you with?

Fred: Oh no, but I appreciate the offer. Once I get that old tin lizzy of mine sold, I'm not going to have any trouble getting in on time. Don't worry about it.

Manager: Well, I am concerned about you, Fred, because you've always been a good employee. I just want you to know that I'm always ready to talk to you if you want to.

Many employees, as well as managers, have been raised with the erroneous belief that you don't take personal problems to work. In the real world, unfortunately, it is not always easy to separate the two. Even if the employee declines an offer of help when it is first made, just the knowledge that the supervisor is willing to talk may open the door to help at a later time.[3]

Many personal problems are beyond the scope of a manager's capacity to help, of course, and will require outside professional help. In many cases, however, if the employee takes the risk of opening up to a friendly manager, just talking about the problem to someone who is willing to listen can be a major source of comfort. It should also be a source of comfort to the manager who is not a professional counselor or therapist to realize that the skill such trained professionals use most frequently in helping their clients is sympathetic listening. The manager does not have to set himself up as a Sigmund Freud to be helpful; just being willing to pay attention to the employee's problem may prove to be of great assistance.

When and How to Refer the Employee

Referring an employee to an outside professional is a judgment call, but there are some sensible guidelines the manager can follow. The following list of behavioral indicators requiring outside intervention is not complete, by any means, but it will serve as a handy checklist for the concerned supervisor.

1. The employee threatens to kill himself or herself or to harm other employees.
2. The employee is despondent and listless for long periods of time or has rapid mood swings from depression to extreme giddiness or elation.
3. The employee complains that he is being persecuted or that others are "out to get him" (when this is not the case).
4. The employee is physically sick much of the time, using all available sick leave and has acetone breath and dilated pupils.
5. The employee is repeatedly caught lying about his or her whereabouts and activities.
6. The employee's motor control and coordination are so poor that he represents a danger to himself and others.

In this short list, a number of causes are possible for each of the behaviors listed, and the supervisor may never know what the actual cause of the behavior is. Persons who are severely hypoglycemic (a blood-sugar disorder), for example, may be mistakenly perceived as drunk.

A note on drunken or drug-affected behavior, if the reader will. When a manager encounters an employee who is obviously under the influence of an intoxicant or mood-altering substance and who is perceived to be a major nuisance to other employees or dangerous, the person should be sent home immediately, preferably in a cab if one is available. The person should be sent home not because he or she is intoxicated, but because he cannot perform his job or is a hazard to himself and others. *Never* attempt to interview or counsel an employee who is drunk or under the influence of drugs. *Do* ask to talk to the person the next morning when he or she has normally detoxified and is highly susceptible to tough-minded intervention.

Referral is also a nonjudgmental process, and it follows the same sequence of steps involved in getting a promise of action from the employee. An early intervention might go as follows:

Manager: Joe, I don't know what the problem is, but you've been down in the dumps for a month now. Do you think you might find it helpful to talk with our EAP counselor Jim Brown? The EAP program is designed for everyone, and it's completely confidential.

For the manager lucky enough to work for an organization with an Employee Assistance Program, or EAP, a source of professional help is right at hand. Because many smaller organizations do not have such a plan, however, the question of who to refer the employee to is somewhat trickier. A logical first person is the organization's physician, if there is one.

If not, or if the supervisor is in doubt as to whom to mention to the employee, the Personnel Department might be genuinely helpful and have several names available. If Personnel can't help, the method of asking around is often useful. This method, as you might expect, consists of asking other managers or reasonably intelligent individuals for the names of agencies or professionals in the community with appropriate programs or skills. If these procedures are of no avail, the employee's physician may also be a source of information and practical help.

While professional help is certainly to be preferred to no help, unfortunately it is not an absolute guarantee of improved performance. Even the best programs for alcohol and drug dependency, for example, have fairly high recidivism or failure rates. Good managerial judgment is involved in the decision as

to how long to retain an employee who shows no signs of progress even after prolonged participation in a program. Although
opinions vary in this area, a workable rule in most situations
would be that if there is no improvement in the employee's performance after six months, termination should be actively considered.

Avoiding the Dependency Trap

Since most of us are filled with the milk of human kindness,
there is nothing that makes us feel better than to give help to a
suffering other. Since most of us have fairly healthy egos, nothing fills us more with pride than the knowledge that we have
helped someone to solve a problem. Unfortunately, as is so often
the case with kind and virtuous acts, there can be an unpleasant
flip side. Witness a well-meaning, kindly manager fall into the
dependency trap, trying to help an employee:

Employee: Gosh, Mr. Smith, I know you've had a lot of experience buying cars, and well, gee, I'm only eighteen
and my old clunker's ready to give up the ghost. I'm
going to have to buy another car, right away, and
I've never bought a car. My dad gave me my old
Ford two years ago. I wonder if you could help me.
Could you tell me what kind of used car I should
buy?

Manager: I'll be glad to help you, Willy. Those little Subarus
make great used cars, and if you just run on down to
Leon's Used Car Sales, on Highway 99, I know he's
got one on the lot right now that'd be right up your
alley. Tell him I sent you.

Employee: Gee, thanks, Mr. Smith. I'm going to go over there
right now.

Manager: Think nothing of it, Willy. Always glad to help.

The perceptive reader has already detected the proverbial self-
inflicted wound in the foot, to be sure.

After the young employee leaves his office, our manager sits
back and feels good. But after little Willy has been back five

more times with different problems, and after the little Subaru turns out to be one of Leon's classic lemons, and the manager is blamed for telling Willy to buy it, the do-good manager probably wishes he had kept his big mouth shut. He has become a father figure of sorts to the young employee, who has neatly transferred responsibility for decisions to his friendly supervisor.

How to give help without making the employee dependent and taking up all your time? Nonjudgmental counseling and helping skills can help the manager avoid the trap. Let's replay the interview with Willy:

Willy: . . . could you tell me what kind of used car I should buy?

Manager: Well, let me ask you something, Willy, do you think it would be worthwhile to try to repair the car you're driving?

Willy: No, I don't think so, Mr. Smith. For one thing, it needs a new transmission, and for a second, it's got so many miles on it that it could have gone to the moon and back. Also, the body's got so much rust, some days I'm afraid I'm going to fall right through the floor. No, it really wouldn't be worth repairing.

Manager: It sounds like you've already decided it isn't worth repairing, Willy. Tell me, how large a car do you need?

Willy: Well, I could get by with a subcompact because mostly I just drive around town and back and forth to work. But boy, I'd really like to buy a full-sized car, like one of those neat Lincoln Continentals. Do you think I could afford a full-sized car, Mr. Smith?

Manager: Well, I guess I'd ask you another question, Willy. How much can you afford to spend on a car?

Willy: Gosh, I've got about three hundred bucks saved up that I could use for a down payment, and I think I could afford to pay about another hundred bucks a month on it. I know old Leon can get me financing if I can make a bit of a down payment. But there's no way I could afford the Lincoln, I guess, with that kind of payment. Guess I'll have to shoot for something a little smaller. I think I'll look at some compacts or subcompacts.

Manager: Sounds like you've made another decision, Willy. Are there any particular models you're interested in?

And so it goes. Willy's questions are answered by questions, questions that ask him to do his own thinking. By the time he leaves the manager's office, he will probably have made his own decision, and more importantly, leave with the feeling that it was *his* decision.

It is this last aspect of helping that is most genuinely helpful, enhancing a person's ability to make decisions about his own life, and thus, become more independent and a more healthy adult. Any manager who is able to promote this type of growth, even though it will cost him some time, will enjoy the long-term satisfaction of having helped develop another self-directed productive employee. Case closed.

STEP 4: GETTING A PROMISE OF ACTION
THAT WILL SOLVE THE PROBLEM

- You take one of the following five actions, depending on the severity of the problem and the employee's willingness to cooperate.

  1. The employee *volunteers* to take action that will clear up the problem.
  2. You *suggest* action to the employee that will solve the problem.
  3. You *ask* the employee to take action to solve the problem.
  4. You *tell* the employee to take appropriate action and explain what action you will have to take if he or she doesn't.
  5. You *spell out the consequences* of not taking action, including termination, if the employee doesn't take action.

- If formal disciplinary action becomes necessary, follow the *sequence of steps* required by your organization and make a genuine *offer to help* before firing the employee.

- When all other interventions fail, you *terminate* the employee. You always terminate because of the employee's *failure to perform* satisfactorily. You terminate because you were *left with no choice*, and you terminate with *regret*, but with finality.

A CONSTRUCTIVE DIALOGUE

Let's stop and take a look at how some of these techniques can be used to solve problems. The following dialogue illustrates how one tough-minded manager and an employee work together to resolve a problem. Notice how the manager helps the employee explore his options by asking questions and listening, all in a nonjudgmental way.

"The Lord of the Laundromats"

Mark Jones sat alone in his office in the headquarters of the Marvelous Midwestern Food Processing Corporation. He was contemplating his meeting the following morning with Fred Brown, an assistant product manager in the Grocery Products Division of MMFPC, and the rather unique problem that Fred posed.

Fred Brown was 45 years old and had been with the company for 22 years. He had started as a stockroom clerk in the Animal Foods Division and worked his way up to assistant product manager after 14 years of service distinguished by hard work, energy, and imagination. His performance reviews had always been excellent, and numerous supervisors had praised him highly over the years for his diligence and loyalty to MMFPC. Fred had intermittently taken courses at two area colleges toward a Bachelor's Degree in Business Administration. However, he had discontinued his college education after the birth of his third child and was still two years short of completing his degree.

Five years ago, three years before Mark became the manager of the Grocery Products Division, Fred had been passed over for promotion to product manager in favor of a woman ten years his junior who had been with MMFPC a mere three years. She, however, had completed her MBA degree at a prestigious private school in the East and had worked for a competitor for two years before being hired as an assistant product manager in the Grocery Products Division. She had had major responsibility for two highly successful dry cereal promotions that had reversed declining sales of two premium brands and had earned a personal letter of commendation from the vice president of marketing for her creativity and enthusiasm in organizing the promotions.

Mark Jones was well aware that Fred was extremely bitter about being passed over in favor of the woman. His dissatisfaction took the form of frequent complaints for a period of about a year, but his job performance continued to be excellent. In the four years that followed, however, a decline in his productivity became apparent. While Fred continued to come to work faithfully, Mark heard through the "grapevine" that Fred had bought a laundromat, and was spending a good deal of time getting it operational.

Over the last three years, Fred added three more laundromats to his chain. His performance ratings continued to be satisfactory, but he was often observed talking on the phone to suppliers and friends, obviously on laundromat business. He missed several meetings regarding new product development strategies, but in general continued to be cooperative when his attendance was required. What became most disturbing about his performance was the fact that he began calling in sick, and during the last year had used 17 days of sick leave.

Mark decided to talk to Fred before what was now a performance problem became a crisis. Three months ago he had attended an in-house training seminar on coping with problem employees, and he had done so with Fred in mind. While he enjoyed the seminar in general, he paid specific attention to what the trainer said about preparing carefully for interviews with Fred. As he sat in his office, he began rehearsing what he was going to say and do the following morning.

At 9:07 the next morning, Mark Jones's office door opened and Fred Brown entered. As Fred closed the door, Mark pleasantly said, "Hi Fred, how are you today? Would you like to have a chair?"

Fred: I'm fine Mr. Jones. Thanks. What's up?
Mark: Fred, you're probably wondering why I asked to meet with you today, and the reason is that I'd like to talk with you about a problem. I know that you've been increasingly active with the laundromats you own and

that the business has been taking up more and more of your time. It looks like you're doing pretty well with the business too, wouldn't you say?

Fred: Well, yes, I have been, thanks. I had some real headaches four years ago, but the cash flow has been positive for a year now. Getting these laundromats under control has been the biggest challenge of my life, I guess.

Mark: I'm glad to hear that you're getting on top of things with them, Fred, because getting a business going can be a real pain, but that's not what I wanted to talk to you about. The problem is that the laundromats seem to be taking up more and more of your time, and we're seeing less and less of you around here. I've been going over your attendance record for the last year, and I notice that you've used seventeen days of sick leave. That's very unusual for you, Fred. You never used to call in sick.

Fred: Are you implying that I'm abusing sick leave, Mr. Jones? I've put in more than twenty-two years with MMFPC, and I've still got over a hundred days of sick leave accumulated. Besides, I had the flu a lot this past winter. You know how sick everyone in the office was with that.

Mark: Sure I do, Fred, and I'm not accusing you of any kind of abuse. But the sick leave is getting to be a problem.

Fred: Well, I guess I have been calling in sick more than usual. I'll bet you think it's because I'm spending time on my laundromats, isn't it? You think I'm calling in sick because I've got an emergency to deal with in one of my laundromats, don't you?

Mark: Fred, I can't be the judge of that. But I do know that the laundromats seem to be your pride and joy.

Fred: Yeah, I guess they are, come to think of it. I mean, I think I've been a pretty damned good employee around here, even after I got screwed out of the product manager's job five years ago when that smart-ass college kid, Sally Randle, got promoted. I should have that job.

Mark: I can understand how disappointed you were about that Fred. And yes, you have been a good employee around here. It just seems to me that your real interest is in the laundromats, and how well they're doing, and I think I can also understand that.

Fred: Yeah, gee, I am kind of proud of how well the business is going. It's taken a lot of hard work to turn it around you know. You know, I didn't realize that I had missed that much time last year. I didn't realize that it was becoming a problem. Does that mean you're going to fire me?

Mark: Far from it, Fred, but it is a problem, and I'd like to talk about what options you think we might have for dealing with it. What do you see as the choices you might have, Fred?

Fred: Well, I'd never really thought of it 'til now, but right off the top of my head I can think of one, I can hire someone part time, maybe fifteen hours a week or so, to help run the laundromats—you know, do collections and routine service, and stuff like that—and I've kind of hesitated to do that because I've always run the show myself, kind of out of my hip pocket, if you know what I mean. But if I hired someone, it wouldn't cost me that much, and it would sure save me a hell of a lot of time. Maybe I should think more seriously about that.

Mark: It sounds like it might be a good option for you. Are there any others?

Fred: Well, you know, there's one thing I've been thinking about a little that I should have asked you about a bit earlier, I suppose. I've got twenty-two years in with the company now, and I've been vested in the pension fund for over seven years. I was just wondering, with the business just starting to pay off and all, what if I decided to take early retirement at the end of the year—what do they call it, a golden parachute—so that my pension could be beefed up a little. I hear that George Williams over in Animal Foods did that last year, and he had about twenty-five years in. You're right, I am more interested in running my business than just about anything else, but I feel real nervous about leaving the company with my pension at its present level. I think I might really be interested in some kind of retirement package, if we could put it together. Do you think that might be possible?

Mark: I think that might be possible, Fred. I'd be happy to contact Personnel to see what might be worked out if you think you're interested.

Fred: Yeah, I think I am interested. Do you think you could look into that? I'd sure appreciate it.

On December 31, 1988, six months to the day after his interview with Mark Jones, Fred Brown resigned from the Marvelous Midwestern Food Processing Corporation. The company donated a full year's salary to his pension fund, and gave him six months of severance pay as a part of his leave-taking package. Fred stopped by Mark's office on his last day to thank him for his help in putting together the package.

ENDNOTES

1. E. Magnuson, "David Burke's Deadly Revenge," *Time*, December 21, 1987, p. 30.

2. Personal communication to the author, July 14, 1985.

3. Alfred Benjamin, *The Helping Interview*, 2nd ed. (Boston: Houghton Mifflin Co., 1974).

Nice-Guy Lesson #7

Nobody likes to fire someone, but nice guys avoid it like the plague.

TOUGH-MINDED MANAGEMENT
GETS THE JOB DONE

The Art of the Salutary Firing, or
Nailing the First Trouble Maker You Find

You have inherited the legacy of a nice-guy manager in an insurance office in the Southeast. Thirty-five complaining, malingering, and nonperforming employees greet you on your first day at work. You cannot believe such chaos: You can literally feel the discontentment as you walk through the door. You rapidly realize, after ten different employees have been through your office to complain about the behavior and work attitudes of other employees, that you're going to have to do something fast simply to save your sanity. That afternoon a thirty-something clerk comes back from lunch, obviously drunk. You fire her the next morning at 9:00 A.M. The whole office cheers. You have become a hero.

In the short and mythical scenario just described, a tough-minded manager has carried out a salutary (and necessary) tough-guy act: firing the first troublemaker he or she comes across in a chaotic and demoralized environment left behind by a lackadaisical nice guy. In such a situation, where employees have never encountered the firm hand of a determined and tough-minded manager, employees are virtually begging for management to take *some* action—almost *any* action—to get things under control, and to get production moving again.

The art of the salutary firing is superficially a tough-guy tactic, but it is more genuinely the appropriate response of a manager who recognizes the critical importance of getting a situation under control, and fast, while simultaneously impressing upon wayward employees that this is a manager who is not afraid to take action. The salutary firing, when appropriately used, can rapidly and dramatically turn around an office environment that has run amok; and make the new manager a virtually mythical figure in the eyes of previously demoralized employees.

As usual, some cautionary notes must be interjected here. What is being called a "salutary firing" in this section is just that: It is an initial disciplinary step designed to put an unproductive organization or group on notice, *not* a prelude to a general blood-letting. In this context, it is *not* just another tough-guy tactic to be followed by still others; but is instead an intelligent managerial maneuver designed to give the tough-minded manager some immediate respect and breathing room, while he or she comes to grips with the whole host of problems inherited from the hapless predecessor.

A second note of caution is that a firing, or stern disciplinary step falling short of that, should not be completely *arbitrary*: That is, there should be some basis in deficient performance to merit the action taken. If a conspicuous and loud troublemaker can rapidly be identified (and many of these persons spring forward in their eagerness to test new management), the salutary firing will be even more effective. Even if such a firing is eventually reversed, the organization and its employees will still have been put on notice that management intends to take action, and this notification is probably more important than the eventual outcome of the actual disciplinary case.

A third note is simply a reiterative one: If a salutary firing is to be carried out, it should be done with efficiency, professionalism, and dispatch. If the decision is made to terminate a particularly troublesome employee to improve morale and put the rest of the employees on notice, *never* renege on the decision to fire. To do so is to invite complete disaster. To do less than you have promised is to reduce credibility forever.

In dealing with problems left behind by chaos-creating nice guys, it is simply not always possible or practical to follow each and every step of the problem-solving model outlined in this book. Nailing a troublemaker, and nailing him fast, however, can give the tough-minded manager the freedom to carry out a more deliberate and calm problem-solving process.

Chapter 8

TYING UP THE LOOSE ENDS

Lowell Loveless, Déjà Vu:

After Lowell leaves his office, the manager picks up a yellow legal pad and makes a short note: "Talked to Lowell Loveless re: Mary's complaint he pinched her. He said it was a misunderstanding. He actually bumped against her accidentally with some binders. Said he would talk to her today and clear it up. Day/Month/Year." He places the pad in a drawer in his desk.

Later that day, he walks down to Mary Reilly's office, and casually asks, "By the way, Mary, did Lowell stop by to see you? After I talked with him, he said he would." Mary replies, "Yes, Mr. Wright, he apologized—said it was a misunderstanding—and that it sure wouldn't happen again. I'm not sure I believe it was a misunderstanding, but he was sure eager to tell me it wouldn't happen again. I'd consider it settled. Thanks for talking to him about it."

Mr. Wright makes a further note on his legal pad regarding his conversation with Mary.

Learning to Document Everything

Making records of conversations with employees would surely qualify as one of the most mundane and least creative activities of management. It is also one of the more time-consuming activities, though one of the most vital we must hastily add, to sustaining effective problem solving in dealing with problem employees who threaten to become chronic cases. Supervisors who fail to document a case adequately may well be left twisting slowly in the wind if they attempt to take formal action against an employee whose performance has been unsatisfactory for a lengthy period of time.

The rule of thumb in documenting problem situations is to document *everything* for *everyone*. The everything rule means every incident of unsatisfactory performance, beginning with relatively minor transgressions, such as habitual tardiness of a few minutes a day, all the way to such major performance problems as an employee being too intoxicated to physically perform his or her job. The everyone rule means that unsatisfactory performance must be documented for each and every employee under the manager's jurisdiction. The reason for this rule is that if formal legal action is taken against an employee, and if he can prove to the satisfaction of the court that his performance failures were documented, but those of other employees were not, the employer will likely lose. Indeed the employee might well have been handed a counter-suit in such a situation, alleging unfair discrimination.

While an informal resolution of a problem situation is still being attempted, records need not be elaborate or formal. So-called anecdotal records, which may often take the form of notes scrawled on the backs of envelopes or on legal pads, will often be admitted as evidence in a legal proceeding if they are dated, signed, and kept in some sort of orderly fashion. When attempts at informal resolution have failed, however, documentation must follow the formal procedures described in the union contract or personnel manual. In a case where it seems likely that there will be an eventual termination, the wise manager will consult the organization's legal department before writing documents such as letters of reprimand.

The underlying theme in documentation, if an expression may be coined, is that an ounce of prevention is worth a pound of cure. Keeping records of employee performance may be tedious and time consuming for the manager, but the eventual payoff will make it well worthwhile.

Time Is of the Essence

Managers everywhere are fond of complaining that problem employees take up most of their time—time that they would much prefer to spend on other tasks or with productive employees. Their complaint is well founded: Dealing with problem employees and the havoc they create, *does* take up a disproportionate amount of time. This fact can easily become another avenue of avoidance, of course. "Gosh, I'd really like to do something about that darned Fred, but I just don't have the time."

Although our focus in this volume has been on the negative aspects of employee behavior, there is a positive side too. When the employee does something well and earns the praise of all around him, the manager should also document this and stick it in the file. The problem-solving manager who habitually makes paper trails in the event that formal disciplinary action becomes necessary is also building a *performance file* for the employee that can become the basis for a method of performance appraisal known as "critical-incidents analysis."

Critical-incidents analysis has been growing in popularity throughout government and industry in the last decade because it is a method of appraising performance that meets two important criteria: It is valid, and it is equitable. The method is really fairly simple, and in its most basic form, the supervisor builds a performance file for the employee in the manner just described, then meets with the employee, preferably twice yearly, or even quarterly, and goes through the contents of the file. An overall rating on a four- or five-point scale can then be determined, often by mutual agreement of manager and employee.

Employees typically respond well to the critical-incidents method because it gives them specific and timely feedback that helps them improve job performance.[1] In this respect, the method is an ideal example of a tough-minded problem-solving technique that helps long-term performance. Managers also enjoy using it, because it also helps them handle the appraisal interview more calmly and it allows them to use *good judgment* in evaluating performance.

While no method of performance appraisal is perfect, and while chickenshit managers frequently avoid the issue altogether, methods like these (particularly when organizational policy *requires* their regular use) tend to get the job done with a minimum of fuss and a maximum of employee participation and cooperation.

Learning to Follow up the Problem-Solving Interview

As you might expect, the problem-solving manager's job has not ended when the employee has promised to take action, and the interview has been documented. The short incident that introduced this chapter is a good example of effective managerial follow-up. The legendary Lowell had promised to talk to Mary Reilly the same day, and the manager followed up to make sure that he had. In this case, the employee was as good as his word, and the incident, for all intents and purposes, could be considered closed.

If for some reason, Lowell had not talked to Mary and another chat with her a couple of days later revealed that he still hadn't, another talk with Lowell would now become necessary:

Manager: Lowell, I was talking with Mary Reilly about an hour ago, and she told me you still haven't talked with her about the incident by the water cooler. You're going to follow up on that, aren't you?

Lowell: Gosh, I'm sorry, Ms. Wright. I guess I've been procrastinating on that—been a little embarrassed about it actually—but I'll take care of it today. Think I can word things a bit better now that I've had a little time to think about it. Thanks for reminding me.

The manager has now essentially *asked* the employee to take the action that he volunteered and if additional follow-up steps should prove to be necessary, they follow the same sequence of steps outlined earlier. The manager makes increasing use of his or her authority to get action.

Following up is another essential problem-solving technique, and like documenting everything, it tends to be tedious and time-consuming. It is also understandably frustrating when the manager discovers that the employee is procrastinating or being evasive, and the temptation to give the employee a little old-fashioned hell can be almost irresistible. The tough-minded problem-solving manager, as always, *will* resist such juvenile urges and remain composed, calm, and professional.

Games Employees Play

Many problem employees are not only very adept at hiding and compensating for their poor performance, they are also highly skilled at *managing the manager*: They play cunning psychological games that exploit the manager's weaknesses, and keep him or her on the defensive, while they continue to get away with murder. The determined problem-solving manager can rapidly learn to identify basic employee games, some of which are listed below, and cope with them effectively. It is always disconcerting, however, how rapidly a determined employee can come up with new and creative games to disrupt the work environment. In any event, on to some really basic games.

"I'm Gonna Huff and Puff and Blow Your House Down." This is the "boy-am-I-mad-at-you" game, also known as the temper tantrum. The employee comes in late and rather than slink shamefully to his desk, he scowls and glares at everyone in the area, particularly the manager. Sometimes the anger originates elsewhere (a fight with the spouse that morning, for instance) but often it is a shrewd tactic designed to intimidate the nice-guy manager and make him feel guilty ("What did I do to make him so mad?"). Coping with this game is not easy because most of us respond to anger with anger, which is exactly what the employee is counting on. The manager should stay as calm and adult as he can, talk to the employee *now*, but schedule the interview for *later*. If the employee rants and raves during the interview, the manager can say, "I'm sorry, I'm not going to talk to you when you're acting like this, so I'm terminating our conversation now, but I'm going to talk to you later, when you're more calm." This lets the employee know that: (a) his anger is not getting him anywhere, and (b) he's still going to have to face the problem later. Many employees become calm very quickly when the manager calls a halt to the huff-and-puff game.

"I'm Gonna Provoke a Confrontation." This game usually involves a demand that another employee be brought in "so we can settle this thing right now." The demand to bring in the other employee is sometimes motivated by a genuine desire to see the problem solved, to be sure, but more often it will represent an attempt to obscure the real problem in the smoke of the fiery

battle that is sure to ensue. An employee who is guilty as sin (excuse the momentary lapse into judgmentalism here) will often use the confrontation as a means of intimidating the other employee. Many managers earnestly believe that bringing the employees together is the only way to settle the problem, but this belief is, in a word, wrong. If the employee demands to see the other employees, the problem-solving manager should say something like, "That won't be necessary, Fred. I want to talk to you about the problem now, and I'll talk to Sally later." This firm assertion of authority lets the employee know, again, who the manager is, and how the problem will be handled.

A highly defensive or gamy employee might respond to the supervisor's statement of the problem with an angry statement like, "Are you accusing me of pinching her?" The nonjudgmental response to such an assertion should be something like, "No, I'm certainly not accusing you. I don't know what happened, but there's a problem here I'd like to see cleared up."

"I'm Gonna Throw You a Curve Ball." The curve ball may or may not be a game, but it always represents an unexpected development in the problem that may throw the manager off guard. In the Loveless case, the curve ball could take the form of an indignant response from our industrious auditor, such as, "There's no way I pinched her. She's just making this up to get back at me for bawling her out in front of her friends yesterday." At this point, the manager has no way of knowing whether or not he is telling the truth, and at this point, it doesn't matter. The manager must simply remember to stay in the nonjudgmental problem-solving role, to the best of his or her ability, and play out the rest of the interview as before. In this case, however, even if Lowell is telling the truth, the action step might be exactly the same as before: He's going to talk to her in an attempt to get it cleared up. When the curve-ball strategy is used in an attempt to manipulate the manager, it is an attempt to shift responsibility to someone else and to persuade the manager to side with the curve-balling employee. The best way for the manager not to get hooked (or struck out, in this analogy) is precisely to stay in the tough-minded role, and neither agree nor disagree with the employee. Even if the employee asks directly, "Don't you agree with me?," the manager should still say neither "yes" nor "no," but instead, something like, "I'm not here to judge either of you, or take sides, and I don't honestly know what

happened between you two; I just want to get this problem cleared up."

"I'm Gonna Bring In the Union Steward." The much-feared confrontation with the dreaded union steward seems to be at hand. Upon hearing the statement of the problem, the employee immediately demands that the union steward be called in. If the manager stays in the nonjudgmental problem-solving role, however, there will not be a confrontation; the union representative can actually help in getting action to solve the problem. Employees frequently want a representative present during the interview because they are afraid they are going to be punished by a tough-guy manager. When the union steward sees and hears the manager using nonjudgmental skills, and in particular, hears the manager make a genuine offer to help the employee, he will often urge the employee to take action to solve the problem. In the author's experience as a consultant, at least a dozen different managers who have held problem-solving interviews in the presence of an employee representative report that the third party actually facilitated rather than obstructed the interview.

Interviewing the Minority or Female Employee

While minority groups and women have at long last made inroads in American management, it is still largely the province of the white male. In most industries, well over 90 percent of all executives are males of the caucasian persuasion, while most representatives of minorities or women are still subordinate employees. The usual situation that occurs, therefore, when a problem arises and ethnic background or sex is a variable, is that a white manager finds himself the interviewer.

This fact can readily become yet another cop-out for the determined chickenshit manager, which also contains all of the elements of self-fulfilling prophecy:[2] A generally negative judgment about another sex or group that through our own actions we make true. With regard to a black employee who is not performing satisfactorily, for example, the trembling manager avoids his responsibility by declaring, "Oh my goodness! He's black, and he'll get violent and hurt me if I try to do anything." With regard to a woman, it's "Oh dear, she'll get emotional and cry in my office if I try to talk to her."

Since the typical minority or female employee is not stupid, he or she will take advantage of the nice-guy manager in exactly the same way as any other employee would, but probably with a little more enthusiasm and zest. Most minority persons and women, if they were to be totally honest, probably feel they are entitled to a little "get-even" time after the long history of past discrimination in our society.

In any event, motives and history aside, what does the manager do when a problem arises in such a situation? The answer, of course, is to interview the employee using exactly the same tough-minded problem-solving techniques that would be used with any other person. In addition, however, the manager should, to the best of his ability, make no assumptions whatsoever about the possible behavior or motives of the employee.

The cunning employee, however, may attempt to bring in race or sex as a variable. If the auditor we have been discussing, Mr. Loveless, were Hispanic, for example, he might say something like the following in response to the manager's statement of the problem:

Lowell: You're really just making this up, aren't you, because I'm Latin, and you've got it in your head that I'm some sort of Latin lover?

Manager: Your ethnic background really has nothing to do with it, Lowell. I asked to talk with you because I had a complaint that you pinched her at the water cooler, and that's all I want to talk to you about. Can you tell me what you recall about that?

In this case, the manager gets the interview right back on track, by returning firmly to the statement of the problem.

If a woman were the manager, in the case of the ardent auditor, a phenomenon that is now more common, she might well be expected to have some strong feelings about a case of suspected sexual harassment. Her task would naturally be the same as the male manager's: To as great an extent as possible, stay in the role of the tough-minded problem solver and avoid accusations like the plague. The following statement would not get the interview off to a promising start, for example:

134

Ms. Manager:	I've just had a complaint from Mary Reilly, Mr. Loveless, that you pinched her while she was standing at the water cooler. She told me she didn't encourage you in any way, and I believe her. You guys have been pulling this kind of crap for generations and by God it's going to stop. You get right down to her office now, and you apologize, you hear me? And if this happens again, I'm going to have your head, understand? Now get moving.

Although the tough guy in this example is a woman, the same result is to be expected: Loveless will hustle to obey in the short run, but because he feels unfairly judged and has been humiliated, he will undoubtedly seek revenge in the long run.

The general rule for the manager in a case where race or sex might lead to strong feelings or extreme defensiveness is to take a little more time to prepare for the interview. Settle down. Think about what you are going to say. No matter how hateful the behavior of the employee might have been, remember that your role is to solve the problem and that you will not rectify a long history of societal injustice in one interview. Put away your gun.

A final comment on self-fulfilling prophecy: When an employee runs amok due to managerial inaction, and where race or gender is involved, the resulting behavior confirms the prejudicial prophecy. "See, look at that lazy and worthless Larry. I knew we shouldn't have hired a black guy for the job." This sort of outcome not only hardens and deepens feelings of antagonism and prejudice, it also conveniently overlooks the fact that the manager abdicated his or her responsibility for coping with the employee's performance. The history of avoidance, unfortunately, was not written in a day and will probably not be rewritten in a day.

STEP 5: LEARNING TO DOCUMENT EVERYTHING AND FOLLOWING UP THE INTERVIEW

- You document *every* incident of unsatisfactory performance for *every* employee. In the early stages of a problem, *anecdotal records* are valuable and easy to keep.

- Document each interview in summary form, including the *promise of action* the employee makes.

- You *follow up* the interview in an attempt to ensure the employee carries out the actions he or she has promised.

- Stay alert for *basic employee games* that are usually an attempt to distract you from effective problem-solving measures.

- In an interview with a woman or minority employee (or with a man if you are a woman manager), where you might be *anxious* or *prejudiced*, follow basic tough-minded interviewing procedures, but take more *time* to prepare the interview so you can remain calm and objective.

A CONSTRUCTIVE DIALOGUE

Let's stop for a minute and look at a problem-employee situation. The following dialogue illustrates how one "manager" learned to manage a problem employee with tough-minded management techniques in order to get a job done.

"Jerry the Drunken Carpenter"

In 1973, Gregory Gaertner bought a nineteenth-century two-story red brick house in St. Louis for the sum of $1,000. Despite its age, the house was structurally sound, and had been occupied until just a few months earlier when its owner had died. Gaertner had no difficulty acquiring the house from the owner's heirs, who were well aware that the house was located in a declining inner-city neighborhood.

On the south side of the building was a wooden two-story porch, complete with ornate railings, that was about to tumble into the street. The support pillars of the porch had completely rotted away, and the railings and decking were literally holding the structure together. Gregory realized that he would soon need the services of a good carpenter if he were to salvage the porch before a city building inspector condemned it and forced him to demolish it. He began making inquiries of other friends who were restoring old buildings, asking them if they knew of a carpenter who might be available, and who would also be relatively cheap and dependable.

George Smith, one of Gregory's old acquaintances soon came up with a name. "Give Jerry Fryer a call, Gregory. Here's his number. Now, he's a good carpenter, and a pretty decent handyman, but he likes his beer, and you've got to watch him. I've been paying him eight bucks an hour for things like rebuilding porches." Gregory thanked George, and immediately called Jerry Fryer. Within an hour, they were standing next to Gregory's building and discussing the job. Fryer seemed sober and sensible, and told Gregory he could repair the porch, not including time spent to purchase materials, in about five days, and that the job would involve twenty-five hours of labor. Gregory told him to begin immediately.

Three weeks later, the porch had still not been completed. Gregory had advanced Jerry $100 at the carpenter's request, and Jerry promptly disappeared for a week after he received the money. When he reappeared, and finally began working on the porch on a sunny Tuesday morning, he told Gregory that he had gone to Memphis to see a sick relative. It was Jerry who looked ill, however; he was unshaven, and his face looked red and puffy. Nonetheless, he went to work on the porch.

During the next two weeks, Gregory noticed that Jerry came and went at irregular hours. The work moved ahead slowly, even though the weather continued to be fine. At the end of the third week, Gregory finally told Jerry that he would have to finish the porch by the end of the following week if he were to count on receiving the final payment on the job. Jerry muttered, complained, and mumbled, but magically and mysteriously, despite additional absences during normal working hours, the job was completed within hours of the deadline that Gregory had decreed. After Jerry had picked up an additional $100 from Gregory, he rushed off, saying he had to keep an appointment with another developer. Gregory thanked him, and in turn rushed off to see George Smith.

As Gregory began telling the tale of the prolonged reconstruction of the porch, he noticed his friend's pained expression:

Gregory: What's that awful look all about, George? You look like you just swallowed a watermelon whole.

George: Greg, I'm sorry. I should've warned you about that Jerry, and how to handle him. He's a booze hound, you know, and the minute you give him a nickel, he'll run down to the nearest tavern and blow it. I should've warned you.

Gregory: Yeah, I noticed that as soon as I gave him a hundred bucks up front, he blew town for a week. Said he had to go to Memphis to see a relative.

George: Memphis, hell. He was right here all the time, I'm sure, probably in Gene Cole's tavern, getting himself blown away. I should've warned you never to give him money up front. I had to learn that lesson myself the hard way two years ago. Jerry can be a darned good handyman, but you've got to handle him just right. You can't treat him like he's a grown-up, unfortunately.

Gregory: What do you mean by that, George?

George: Well, with these construction guys, booze is usually a problem. But with Jerry, it's a big problem, and so you've got to treat him differently. For starters, never, *never*, advance him money on a job. Not even if he begs you, or tells you that he needs fifty bucks to buy food for his sister who's starving to death. He'll feed you story after story if you let him. Also never advance him money to buy materials: He'll immediately run out and spend it all on beer.

Gregory: Well, at least I did one thing right. I made sure I bought all the materials for the porch.

George: Don't kick yourself, Greg, at least he got the job done for you before Christmas. I can give you some tips for handling him in the future, if you'd like, so that he gets things done on schedule. Are you interested?

Gregory: Go ahead, George, shoot.

George: Well, it's usually Jerry you end up wanting to shoot if you let him get out of hand. Here's what I do with him when I want to use him on a job. First I never give him a job that's too big for him to handle. Nothing that ever lasts more than a month. Second, as I just said, I never advance him cash. And third, we walk through the job together and figure out how many hours it's going to take him. And we make it a firm figure; no additions to the hours. That's another game he likes to play: find some complications on the job, and double the hours on you. That's why it's real important you take a lot of time at the front end, and walk through the whole thing carefully. Use a real fine-tooth comb. 'Cause you know what it's like in rehab, with things popping up all the time. If there *is* something out of the ordinary, you can budget it separately. But you want to make that the exception, not the rule.

Gregory: Well, that's another thing I got right. We set the porch at twenty-five hours, and I stuck to it.

George: Good for you, Greg. The other thing I do with Jerry is I make him sign a contract on every job, and then I countersign. Before I draw up the contract, he and I agree on a reasonable amount of time to complete the job, even allowing for lousy weather. I then put the completion date in the contract, and then I just deduct a sum from the amount of the contract for every day after the completion date, if the job's not done. I usually knock ten percent off for each day late. The first time I did this with him, it got to be a real comic opera. He was rebuilding a cornice for me, blew the deadline completely, and tried to tell me he was down with the flu. I could tell just by looking at him that he had the Budweiser flu. Anyway, he wraps the job up a week late, and according to the contract he has about sixty bucks coming to him. I pay him, and he breaks down crying like a little kid. Begs me to give him the full amount, curses me when I don't, and then cries again. I feel guilty as hell, of course, but I stick to my guns.

Gregory: Good for you, George. Did that teach him a lesson?

George: Yeah, it did. He did a nice job on the cornice, by the way. He's a fine carpenter when he wants to be, as I'm sure you noticed. So a few weeks later I call him on another job—this time I want an interior wall removed—and after he's through sulking for awhile, he comes on over, and we set up another contract. This time, though, I tell him I'll give him a five percent bonus for each day that he gets the job done ahead of schedule, if the work meets my standards. His eyes light up, and he gets to work, and I mean pronto. Busts his tail for a week and a half, and brings the wall in three days ahead of schedule. Took a lot of pride in the sucker too. Now mind you, the minute I paid him, he was off on a toot, but he was also back three days later, sober, asking if he could pick up another job with me. Said I was a real hard-ass, but I was a fair boss to work for. And he's been

140

pretty good for me ever since, but I can't trust him with an open-ended deal, or put him on straight hours. He'd just immediately abuse the set-up, and I'd end up having to hover over him like a mother hen. And I just don't have time to do that. So the moral is, set up the contract and have the guts to stick to it.

Gregory: I appreciate the input, George. I think I know how to handle him for the future.

ENDNOTES

1. See John Ivancevich and William Glueck, *Foundations of Personnel* 3rd ed. (Plano, Texas: Business Publications, 1986): 276-318, for an excellent discussion of performance appraisal.

2. Robert Rosenthal and Lenore Jacobsen, *Pygmalion in the Classroom: Teacher Expectations and Pupils' Intellectual Development* (New York: Holt, Rinehart, and Winston, 1968).

Nice-Guy Lesson #8

Games the whole office can play!

TOUGH-MINDED MANAGEMENT
GETS THE JOB DONE

The Concept of a Last-Chance Agreement or Contract

Regrettably, the drop-out or recidivism (failure) rate in even the best-managed drug- and alcohol-abuse treatment programs varies anywhere from 40 to 70 percent. Nothing is more frustrating for the tough-minded manager than successfully referring an employee for treatment, having the employee complete some or all of the treatment, then return to a progressive and destructive pattern of substance abuse. Nothing stretches the limits of managerial good will, the limits of human sympathy, and the limits of human patience more than the chronic drug or alcohol abuser whose behavior does not improve. Many of these cases drag on for years, despite the apparent cooperation and sincerity of the affected employee, and despite the genuine desire of everyone involved to help the employee with his or her problem.

Rather than let things drag on indefinitely, and painfully, creative organizations around the country have developed and begun using something called the "Last-Chance Agreement" or contract, which puts the chronically nonperforming employee on notice that his or her employment will be terminated, or that severe disciplinary action will be taken, if he doesn't shape up. This type of agreement, as we have already noted, is most frequently used in cases of substance abuse, but its applicability is not limited to such cases.

While the wording of such documents will vary from organization to organization, the attached agreement developed by the Bureau of Water Works of the City of Portland, Oregon, is a good example of such an agreement. In this agreement, an employee involved with substance abuse is explicitly required to complete a prescribed treatment program, as described in Clause

143

i: "[Employee] agrees that his failure to complete the prescribed program by Kaiser Permanente may result in his immediate dismissal." The consequences of failure to perform are spelled out clearly and simply in this short statement.

An interesting feature of the Portland Water Bureau document is that the union agent signed the document, along with the supervisor and the employee. As we pointed out earlier, an employee union will normally cooperate fully with a tough-minded managerial approach designed to help the employee, and this is the case with the Portland agreement. Responsible union representatives not only share management's concern for employee welfare, they also realize that a chronic case of nonperformance will detract significantly from the union's image. Enough said.

A cautionary note on such agreements. While they spell out the consequences for the employee's continued failure to perform, and are signed voluntarily (although usually with the threat of severe disciplinary consequences if the employee does not sign), to the author's knowledge, there have yet been no court tests of such documents. While their legality, in a general way, is probably not in doubt, the prudent employer will ask the legal department, or a competent outside attorney, to review any such document before executing it.

CITY OF

PORTLAND, OREGON

BUREAU OF WATER WORKS

LAST-CHANCE AGREEMENT

BETWEEN

PORTLAND WATER BUREAU

AND

(EMPLOYEE)

a) It is acknowledged that (employee) has not fulfilled the terms and conditions of the Continuation of Employment Agreement between City of Portland Water Bureau and (employee) dated (month, day, year).

b) (employee) voluntarily agrees to an examination by the physician of his choosing to determine his physical ability to perform the duties of his position. The results of the said examination will be used to determine his suitability for that position.

c) (employee) voluntarily agrees to an evaluation by Kaiser Permanente to determine the need, if any, for medical treatment.

d) (employee) agrees to allow communication between (counselor), Kaiser Permanente and the treating physician(s) by signing the attached medical release(s) and filing the same with the appropriate practitioner(s). Any information provided will be held in strict confidence. (employee) further agrees that communication needs to take place between (counselor) and the treatment program that he shall enter into for the purpose of ensuring his attendance and completion. He thus agrees to allow written reports signed by the treatment center every two (2) weeks after beginning treatment to be mailed to (counselor). These reports will be for the sole purpose of indicating (employee) attendance and progress in the treatment program and shall be placed in his personal file.

e) (employee) agrees to submit to treatment if recommended by the practitioners and understands that the cost of the examinations and/or treatment program will be paid for by his health benefit plan or by himself. The City of Portland will make every effort to see that the existing health benefit program offered by the City on behalf of the employees will cover the cost of any required treatment.

f) (employee) agrees that he will arrange appointments as much as possible for after work hours and weekends; however, the use of his Sick Leave account for attendance at the appointments will be acceptable.

g) (employee) understands that he will be subject to the terms of this agreement until he completes the program as prescribed by Kaiser Permanente.

h) (employee) understands that he will remain on Sick Leave probation for a minimum of nine (9) months from the date of this agreement.

i) (employee) understands that he must meet the expectations placed upon all Water Bureau employees, which includes the need for consistent attendance and adherence to the bureau's reporting policy. (employee) agrees that his failure to complete the prescribed program by Kaiser Permanente may result in his immediate dismissal.

The parties to this document agree that if, after completion of the treatment program, (employee) finds that he is ill and requires use of Sick Leave, he shall notify the Operations Supervisor to whom he is assigned. Should he be unable to contact that supervisor, he shall contact any other Operations

146

Supervisor or the Scheduling Coordinator. It will not be acceptable for (employee) to advise the emergency crew that he needs Sick Leave. (employee) understands that failure to comply with this requirement will be cause for a separate disciplinary action.

j) (employee) understands and agrees that a written report at the conclusion of the program indicating his progress, attendance, and a schedule of follow-up treatment (if it involves treatment during working hours) shall be prepared by Kaiser Permanente and mailed to (counselor). The document will then be placed into (employee's) personnel file.

k) The parties hereto agree that the successful completion of the program will result in the removal of all documentation from (employee's) personnel file concerning this action. After one year from the date of successful completion of the program herein described, documentation concerning any and all disciplinary actions shall be removed from (employee's) file, providing the conditions of this document have been fulfilled.

AGREED TO and SIGNED THIS _____
day of (month, year) by:

_____
(employee)

_____
(director, Operations &
Maintenance Division)

_____
(Business Agent, AFSCME Local)

Chapter 9

THE TOUGH-MINDED PROBLEM SOLVER TAKES ON THE WORLD

It is the year 2001 and the last known American living in Lebanon, Dr. Feckless Fateful, a professor of astrology at the Peace Institute of Lebanon, has just been taken hostage by an extremist group. The group announces that unless $3 billion worth of sophisticated military hardware is immediately sent to the revolutionary Muslim government of Saudi Arabia, it will kill Dr. Fateful. Dr. Fateful's family appeals directly to the president, Mr. Halfway Heartless, to send the hardware forthwith.

Heartless confers with his trusted advisors on the National Security Council, then announces that no deal will be made under any circumstances. He adds, "We've learned something after forty years of dealing with these punks," and sends heartfelt condolences to the Fateful family. The extremists make repeated threats to kill the professor, then release him unharmed after a year.

Dr. Fateful's family castigates the administration for its "sloth and inaction." Mr. Heartless is re-elected to a second term in a landslide victory in the fall of 2004.

While the focus of this modest volume has been on dealing effectively with the problem employee, other problems can be dealt with equally effectively using a tough-minded approach. Tough-minded management is much more than just a practical method for coping with nonperforming employees; it is also a philosophy for effective living. The mythical short case that introduced this chapter illustrates a tough-minded approach to a problem that has bedeviled a succession of presidents, and that we are finally approaching more effectively. Other societal problems can be dealt with equally expeditiously by the determined application of tough-minded principles, but let us deal with the issue of terrorism first.

We have just begun to learn, it would seem, a lesson in chickenshit avoidance that was forced upon the British a generation ago: When terrorists are appeased or bribed, they don't cease terrorist activities; in fact, they become even more aggressive. The current rounds of hostage taking in the Middle East are a sad consequence of a policy of appeasement. Whatever their other failings, terrorists are bright enough to understand that their activities are paying off, either in terms of arms payments or the release of jailed terrorists, and they will go right on taking hostages until we have the guts as a nation to adopt a tough-minded policy that will eventually end it.

The adoption of a tough-minded policy to manage terrorism (no payoffs, period) will have some costs, particularly in the short run. Innocent Americans will almost certainly be killed. There will be an outcry from their families and friends that we have not done enough or tried hard enough to seek their release. Moralists will advise us that we have lost all respect for human life and are becoming as callous as the Soviets. But in the long run, of course, fewer Americans will be killed.

Those Americans who choose to continue living in areas of great danger such as Lebanon, where their safety cannot be assured, must be treated as adults who have made a conscious and rational decision. The consequences of this decision must be clearly spelled out: If you are taken hostage, no effort will be made to seek your release. There must be no deviation from this policy.

Further, it may be necessary to engage in selective and intelligent military action against known terrorists or against nations that have demonstrably supported terrorism. Within our limits, terrorism will be punished. For their parts, the Israelis and the Russians have long understood this, made it an instrument of tough-minded policy, and communicated it forcibly to terrorist groups. We are just now reaching a similar place.

In our current national debate over how to deal with terrorism, it is interesting and predictable that we are more actively considering and using tough-minded (and yes, tough-guy) approaches and policies to cope with the problem. As the failure of the nice-guy approach has become more and more obvious, and the entire issue less partisan, the overwhelming issue has become the search for a policy that works, and thus, the turn to tough-minded tactics, accompanied by a sad recognition that such a policy will not be without its costs. It is not always a joy being the major player in an international political struggle. The British have had their Munich; it is to be hoped that we can avoid ours.

Drugs, Drugs, and More Drugs

While various hostage crises continue to excite us on the international scene, the great American drug crisis agitates us at home. There can be little question that drug abuse is a serious problem throughout the land, and that drug use is fairly common in the workplace. The problem has been exacerbated recently by the widespread use of the highly concentrated, and sometimes lethal, form of cocaine known as "crack."

The problem has led to a variety of proposed solutions, several of which seem to fall into the tough-guy category. Many of the proposals for random drug testing of students, athletes, and employees in a variety of occupations fit this description and are already being attacked by civil libertarians as representing a fundamentally unconstitutional invasion of privacy. It is likely that the courts will strike down many of the random-testing plans that management attempts to impose upon employees without negotiated consent.

The tough-minded problem-solving approach to this very real dilemma does involve negotiation, of course. In a problem-solving sequence, it must first be recognized that the problem is real and that it will not spontaneously disappear. It must be acknowledged, secondly, that when there is no reasonable basis for suspecting an employee of drug abuse (i.e., when the employee's performance continues to be satisfactory), then random testing will lead to a host of legal actions to block its use. Thirdly, the right of the public to feel secure and confident about its safety in highly visible and sensitive industries such as the airline industry must also be considered.

The management process that is already emerging in such industries is precisely the tough-minded negotiation of testing and preventative programs that everyone can live with. One of the realistic characteristics of a negotiated solution, built around consensus processes, is that no one is going to be entirely happy with it. The merits of specific plans aside, the only programs that are likely to be workable and effective in the long run are those that have generated broad consent within the organization and are clearly focused on dealing with the problem.

In our society, interestingly enough, when any problem such as drug abuse has been identified as a "crisis," and the problem can no longer be avoided, the first round of solutions proposed for dealing with it generally take a tough-guy, authoritarian approach. These often have a good deal of popular appeal, which is normally short-lived because they promise a quick fix for the problem. Once the initial hysteria generated by the crisis mentality begins to subside, however, more sober programs (pun intended) begin to emerge that have more effective problem-solving characteristics.

The most compelling and mortifying historical example of our adoption of a tough-guy policy as a first means of dealing with a "crisis" was the forced evacuation of Japanese Americans from the West Coast to concentration camps in interior states in the spring and summer of 1942. One hundred and ten thousand aliens and citizens—adults and children of Japanese ancestry— were forcibly relocated from their lifetime homes even though "no charges were ever filed against these persons and no guilt was ever attributed to them."[1] Stories were circulated after the bombing of Pearl Harbor that Japanese residents of Hawaii were involved in the bombing, and that Japanese in Oregon, California, and Washington were preparing to undertake a program of mass sabotage. This led to a strong regional demand for relocation.

More than forty years later, feature stories appear yearly in our major newspapers about the evacuation and its consequences. Evacuees and their descendants continue to file lawsuits, even though the relocation was carried out with the full consent and enabling legislation of all levels of government. It is perhaps a tribute to our lingering feelings of guilt about the injustice of this action, as well as to the persistent and articulate reminders of Japanese Americans, and to the general folly of using Hitlerian tactics in a great democracy, that the evacuation is still so much a part of the American conscience. And, at long last, the wheels of justice have turned, and reparations to those Japanese Americans are now being made.

The Check Is in the Mail

A more mundane domestic problem generates several million lies a year in America. This, of course, is the problem of the past-due payment on the old installment loan. The American economy has been stimulated and lubricated by the generous and widespread use of consumer credit, to be sure, but the downside of easy credit is bills that are tough to pay. Most of us have experienced the problem of having to deal with a payment that we just can't make right now. The resulting guilt produces avoidance. Calls from the lending institution are not returned. When the call can't be avoided, the creditor is told the check is in the mail.

While dealing with unpaid bills is unpleasant for everyone, there *is* an alternative to lying and avoidance. This involves calling the creditor, telling him or her that we are having financial headaches, and proposing partial payments or rescheduled payments on the balance of the loan or bill. Most creditors are happy (and surprised!) when debtors call them, and while they may not be overjoyed about partial or delayed payments, they will generally accept such proposals.

This problem-solving approach has the simultaneous function of reducing the stress of guilt and avoidance and increasing the respect of the creditor. Hopefully, of course, the revised payment schedule can be met and cash-flow problems dealt with. This is not in any way proposed as another quick fix: The long-term solution lies in managing the debt burden intelligently, which is not always easy in a society that encourages high levels of individual indebtedness.

The Power and the Pain of Courage

In the hours before the doomed flight of the space shuttle Challenger, NASA Flight 51-L, two courageous rocket engineers at Morton Thiokol, Inc., raised loud and persistent voices against the launch, arguing that cold temperatures at Cape Canaveral had rendered the safety seals on the rocket booster dangerously unsafe. Despite repeated attempts by their employer and NASA to stifle their dissent, they went public with their complaints and criticisms after a horrible explosion destroyed the shuttle and its crew of seven, which included civilian grade-school teacher Christa McCauliffe.

The two engineers, Allan J. McDonald and Roger Boisjoly, later testified before the presidential commission that was appointed to investigate the disaster, and repeated their earlier criticisms. The reward for their tough-minded courage in speaking the truth was that Thiokol management stripped them of many of their responsibilities and took away their staffs. McDonald's authority in the company was restored, however, after the presidential commission expressed outrage at the way he had been treated. He is now a spokesman for Thiokol and its newly redesigned boosters.

Boisjoly has never entirely recovered from the experience and has told friends that it would be too painful for him to ever work on the shuttle again. He is now on the "long-term disability" list at Thiokol. Both men, however, have stated repeatedly that if faced with the same choice again, they would speak out again. Both men are in demand as public speakers throughout the country. They are justifiably applauded by their countrymen for their courage and honesty. They are living testaments to the power and to the pain of being tough minded and honest in the face of great organizational pressure. Boisjoly was asked during a speech at MIT if he would ever again risk his career for his conscience. He replied, "My answer is always an immediate 'yes.' I couldn't live with any self-respect if I tailored my action based upon personal consequences."[2]

Three Farm Boys and a Pile of Manure: A Modern Fable

Three farm boys contemplated a large pile of horse manure that had accumulated on their farm. The first boy, who was a nice boy, began crying. "Oh, it's terrible," he said. "That manure smells so bad already, and the smell's just going to get worse. There's nothing we can do about such a big pile of smelly manure. It's just awful, that's what it is."

The second boy, a tough boy, said, "Sure there's something we can do. We can set it on fire, that's what. We'll burn the manure and get rid of it. But of course, then we'll have air pollution here for months and months."

The third boy, a problem-solving boy, said nothing. Instead, he picked up a pitchfork and began digging vigorously into the pile of manure. The other two boys cried, "What are you doing? What are you doing?" "Well," said the problem-solving boy, "With all the horse manure around here, there's got to be a pony in there somewhere!"

This little fable, with all the usual apologies to the authors of the original joke, illustrates the fundamental differences in outlook between nice-guy, tough-guy, and problem-solving managers. The nice guy is pessimistic because he knows he's going to have to live with a pile of manure that's just going to get worse. The tough guy is also a pessimist because he knows that he might get rid of the pile of manure right now, but that air pollution cause by the burning manure will eventually kill him. The problem solver, however, is serenely optimistic because he knows he's soon going to be finished with a pile of manure, have a fine farm fertilized with horse manure, and be riding a pony. This is a fine bottom line for every tough-minded person who has the courage to pitch in and begin solving problems rather than making them worse.

Tough-Minded Management Revisited

If there has been a single message or theme in this short volume, it is a singularly simple and positive one: Most employee problems, and many of life's problems, can be solved by the early and effective use of tough-minded methods. This book has emphasized that taking action is almost always preferable to doing nothing, and that taking tough-minded managerial action will almost always get the manager respect *and* long-term results. It has recognized the simple reality that most managers have had little if any training in how to cope effectively with problem people, but it outlines a step-by-step approach that almost any manager can quickly learn to use effectively in dealing with employee problems. And it has stated implicitly that most of us have far more courage than we sometimes give ourselves credit for.

The psychological skills required in tough-minded problem solving can also be learned by almost every manager. Most of us have the strength and inner resolve to confront problem situations generally, particularly when we take the time to plan what we are going to say and do. Most of us have the wisdom not to prejudge problem situations, or to get sucked into angry confrontations with game-playing employees, particularly when we know how self-defeating such behavior can be. And every manager knows inwardly that problems will only get worse if they are not dealt with *now*, and that the biggest single step on the road to solving an employee problem is to sit down face to face, one on one, and talk about it.

The five separate steps in tough-minded problem solving are practical and easy to use by the determined manager.

1. Setting up a face-to-face meeting with the employee who is not performing satisfactorily, and treating that person courteously and as an adult, is a necessary first step.
2. Stating the problem specifically but nonprejudicially is possibly the most important step in the entire process because so many important things are communicated to the employee without the manager having to say them—that action must be taken, that the employee must take responsibility for doing something or trouble may result, and that the manager is a friend who wants to help solve the problem before it gets worse.
3. Listening to the employee nonjudgmentally, without getting sucked into disagreements or evasions, is important in clarifying the problem and increasing the employee's willingness to cooperate with a friendly but firm manager.
4. Getting a promise of action from the employee that will solve the problem, and provide a basis for documentation, is an important skill in closing the interview.
5. Documenting and following up on every phase of the problem-solving process is a bit of tough-minded management drudgery that can become critically important if formal disciplinary action must be taken.

It is the *outcomes* of tough-minded problem solving, however, that are most rewarding to the courageous manager who is willing to face problems rather than avoid them. Firstly, there is heightened self-esteem on the part of any manager who is willing to face his or her "gutless nice-guy" tendencies, and (to paraphrase an old expression) get going when the going gets tough. Secondly, there is increased respect for the manager, not only on the part of the problem employee, but among all the other employees who are in some way affected by the problem. Thirdly, there are atmospheric changes in the direction of fair weather: The atmosphere of fear and apathy that pervades both nice-guy and tough-guy managerial environments is replaced by one of optimism and trust. Lastly, and most importantly, there is improved performance on the part of all employees who are the beneficiaries of tough-minded management, and improved morale on the part of every person who is a member of an organization that wants to get the job done.

A CONSTRUCTIVE DIALOGUE

The following dialogue profiles a tough-minded manager and describes his tough-minded management philosophy on employee drug and alcohol abuse.

"Jack Snook: Tough-Minded Fire Chief"

Jack Snook became the Fire Chief of District One in Washington County, Oregon, at the age of 36. District One has a force of approximately 165 full-time fire fighters. Shortly after he became Fire Chief of District One, Jack Snook enrolled in the Masters Program in Public Administration offered by Lewis and Clark College, in Portland, Oregon; and he took a course in human resource management taught by the author. The following interview was recorded before the final class of the term, shortly after Chief Snook had conducted an excellent in-class seminar on his tough-minded approach to coping with problems of drug and alcohol abuse among his fire fighters:

Snook: I began my employment in District One in March, 1986. Four years previous to that, I was the Fire Chief in Lake Oswego, Oregon. I spent twelve years prior to that in southern Oregon, working for Jackson County Fire District Three, at which time I went up through the ranks from fire fighter to administrator. One of the things that I think is important is that I have come up through the ranks and worked in every position, and I have been in the fire stations, lived with the firemen and have a real good feel, I think, for their problems and some of the issues because of their schedule and because of the nature of the work that they do.

Gardiner: Jack, I know that fire fighting is an unusually stressful occupation. I'm aware there are periods of relative boredom and inactivity, followed by periods of intense stress when you and your men are actively fighting fires. When you became the Chief in District One, which I understand has a much larger department than Lake Oswego, what problems did you become aware of in the area of drug and alcohol abuse, or chemical abuse, if you prefer that term?

Snook: Actually, I'd probably been prejudiced a bit prior to going to District One. The word was out, particularly among the circle I traveled in, that the administrators—fire chiefs more particularly—was the fact that they did have a significant problem. I heard some horror stories, particularly about salesmen and vendors taking administrators out to lunch and having to physically help them back to the office because they'd had too much to drink. I was advised, even prior to taking the job, that there was a serious problem, particularly at the administrative and support-staff level, prior to my becoming the administrator at the fire district.

Gardiner: So the administrators were part of the party, if you will, Jack. I remember you telling me that at one

	time the fire chief was expected to be a good old boy and go out partying with his men, if not every night after work, at least every Friday, and that sort of thing. You were aware of this custom, I know, and how did you react to that or deal with it?
Snook:	Well, I think first of all the fire service in general has kind of gone through a transition. Historically, the fire chief was the best fire fighter, who endured and stayed around long enough to have seniority and become the lead person, so to speak. Approximately, I would say twelve to fifteen years ago, we started paying more attention to the need for administrative skills and the ability to manage people rather than be a, quote, senior fire fighter. I was pretty much reared in that system, until I realized through education and working with some pretty good people that you had to manage and treat this thing much more like a business than we'd done it traditionally. I've always felt a sense of it in the private sector. I think we can learn a lot from the problems we've had. I'll skip back a bit to what you said regarding the problems with the profession itself. It's actually two-fold. I think you briefly discussed one, and yeah, that's legitimate. The fact is firemen work really strange shifts. They work 24-hour periods. They come in at 8 o'clock in the morning and work until 8 o'clock the next morning. They literally do live with each other in the fire station. That causes significant problems for the family, so one source of primary stress is the fact that it puts a lot of strain, a lot of pressure on relationships, particularly family relationships. The divorce rate is high. There are a lot of problems with the wife and children, the wife being in a position where she really has to handle the domestic issues because the husband is physically disjointed—he's gone—that puts a lot of pressure on the family, and that's obviously one form. Second, which you alluded to, is the fact that you do go from dead still, even asleep, to having to work 110 percent in a matter of seconds. You

never know when you are going to have to give everything you have, and go from a position of relaxation to making critical decisions that affect other peoples' lives. There's tremendous pressure there. So I think those two things put together set the stage for a person looking to some type of release, and a lot of people look to acquire this release from drugs and alcohol.

Gardiner: Apparently when you took over District One, Jack, the attitude toward the use—and abuse—of alcohol and drugs was a relatively permissive one. From what you said, it's been sort of a tradition in fire fighting, and apparently you were determined to change that attitude, weren't you—as a professional manager—and not a beneficiary of the buddy system.

Snook: Right, very permissive and obviously that causes serious problems for management because it's very hard to enforce policies and practices, and those things you would like to instill in a group, if in fact the people that are doing the enforcing are the biggest violators. So it was an impossible situation. You're not going to hold someone else accountable for something you're doing yourself.

Gardiner: Right, so you decided to lead by example.

Snook: You have to lead by example. Coming in from the outside obviously was to my advantage because I had no history. They had no "skeletons in the closet," so to speak, regarding me and my administrative abilities, or my administration in general. So we started out with a clean slate. About the third day on the job, at a staff meeting, I made a clear statement (on drugs and alcohol) so people would understand what my position was, because I suspected that it would be a problem when I would walk in on a lunch, or at a restaurant, and I didn't want my people to feel that I had set them up. I was very firm about this whole situation. So I just advised them, I announced to the whole group that it would not be tolerated, that it did not have a place in the workplace. Everybody was put on notice and if anyone was caught in violation, and we are talking administrative people at this point, I would take very severe action. I implied that I would probably push for termination.

Gardiner: O.K., so you made it very, very clear, Jack, you made it loud and clear that you would not tolerate drinking on the job. You communicated that very forcefully.

Snook: Right, and there were a lot of Cokes ordered at lunch thereafter. Now, we've had situations since—though we really haven't had much of a problem eight to five—where they're going home and then evening activities bring them back in an official status, where we've ended up with problems. We've had people stop at taverns on the way home in staff vehicles, and it's been reported that people go home and come back to assignments under the influence. These types of people we have dealt with through the program we have established in a very firm, and in both of those cases, a very successful manner.

Gardiner: Could you tell me a bit about the program you've established in District One?

Snook: Basically, I think the program starts by having a good employee assistance program. You have to have a foundation to build from, and it's obvious that our employee assistance program—with all the counseling and help that's available—is nice to have available. Now I have a system set up whereby we will, if a person is found to be in violation and there are alcohol- or drug-related circumstances, we call them in, we investigate, we hold a hearing, and if the charges are found to be correct, they're valid, we discipline them very severely. The whole philosophy behind my approach is that I hit them with an awfully big hammer, and if they agree to volunteer to go into an evaluation program, and then rehab if necessary if drugs and alcohol are involved, I'll reduce the size of that hammer significantly.

Gardiner: You're not using a classic or traditional tough-guy

	approach, are you, Jack? You're not just out there to punish them?
Snook:	No.
Gardiner:	I'm very interested in how you use punishment selectively to motivate your men to go into treatment.
Snook:	The whole idea in working with these people—and experts who deal with them also say so—is that you have to get their attention, and they have to feel like they have no other alternatives, that they are caught, they're trapped in a corner, and they are put in a position where they have to step forward, and begin taking appropriate steps. Without exception, I guess, if there's a trap in the whole process, normally and predictably, they will deny the problem, and they will without any reservations volunteer for the evaluation because they honestly—I believe—think they can either fool the system or get through the evaluation without any black marks. Without exception, however, everyone has come back positive. The experts—professionals—who are an important part of this system, identify their problem with them, and then put them into some type of a rehab program. The discipline part of it is that we will severely discipline them, and then we will reduce that significantly if they volunteer to, number one, get into the program, and number two, release all information back to us as to the results of the initial evaluation and as to their progress through the rehab program. If they are successful there, that's where it stops. If they are not successful, then we have an additional step where we reserve the right to go back and exercise the remainder of the original discipline, plus if they are found in the future to violate any procedures, we will come down very firmly and start gearing them out of the organization, and/or, depending on the situation, give them a second chance. But normally, particularly with drugs and alcohol, once you've expended those kinds of monies and time with that person, if they don't demonstrate their ability to shape up the first time, then normally you have a pretty good idea they might not

162

	be salvageable. That's something that a manager has to face too, that you're not going to turn all these people around.
Gardiner:	That's a pretty tough choice for you, isn't it?
Snook:	It's a tough choice, but you are then in a position where you can look yourself, your employee, and more importantly—the organization—in the eye, and say, "We did all we could, within reason, to be fair and firm with this employee." It puts the burden on their shoulders, the employees' shoulders, and that's where it belongs.
Gardiner:	Jack, when you first confront a troubled employee with what you are calling the big hammer, the disciplinary step you are willing to take, do you typically find that a man—or woman—is hostile?
Snook:	Uh huh. No question. I think a manager has to realize that he is going to be resented to the point where employees are going to communicate outright hatred toward you, as a person, as well as a supervisor. They are very angry about the whole situation. Embarrassed, but the emotion shown is anger. But those people that you turn around and salvage will come back to you later and thank you. You have to realize as a manager that you are doing what has to be done, and you are making decisions for them because they are really not in a position to make good decisions in their state. They are not responsible, but they will come back later, after rehabilitation, those who have made it through rehabilitation, and thank you. They will also indicate they wish that this had happened years ago, because they realize now that they have wasted a good part of their life with this dependency, and they will become some of your better employees.
Gardiner:	Isn't that interesting, Jack! I find it particularly interesting that your men are telling you that they wish you had come along and been as tough minded as you've been, much, much earlier. I suppose you get to listen to a lot of excuses, and a lot of lying, in dealing with these problems.
Snook:	Sure, they will admit they know most of the tricks.

Most of them will admit that we enable them, we make it easy—most managers—because we buy in and even help them make excuses sometimes. Yeah, they are experts at deception, that's part of the whole situation with people who are involved with drugs and alcohol. It sort of goes with the territory. Different people will behave in different ways. The majority will have the classic, typical pattern: The work record will deteriorate, they'll be very emotional when they shouldn't be, they will have poor work results, relationships around the workplace will deteriorate, et cetera. They will have unusual behaviors like brushing their teeth four or five times a day, or chewing gum when you normally wouldn't be, staying away from groups, shying away from conversations. There are others who will look and act like model employees until they go too far with it.

Gardiner: So it's not always obvious that a person's performance is deteriorating. When do you first intervene in most of these cases?

Snook: We'll normally intervene during the performance evaluation process, and will suggest to them that they may have a problem. Almost without exception, and I'm here to tell you through experience, there will be absolute denial. They will tell you I may drink socially, or socially may do this or that (drug), but I don't have a problem. That's usually the last you'll hear of it. That won't be enough to change behavior: Normally, it will not make a person get assistance, or take care of a problem. Normally within a year, after it becomes obvious there is a problem and there's a denial, they will do something at the workplace that will be a cause for disciplinary action and that's when you have the ability to step in and force them to get involved in a proactive program.

Gardiner: Good, Jack. Another question related to this, or two questions really. First, do you feel you're making progress in this whole area in District One, and second, how much of your time does it take on a day-

	to-day, or weekly, basis to cope with this type of performance problem.
Snook:	I think that first of all there's no question that we are making progress. We have a minimum of six, what I would consider to be good to excellent performers, who are alcoholics. They have gone through rehabilitation and are sober at this time. So yes we are making progress. I'm not here to tell you that we are 100 percent successful. I would guess that probably—if I were to grab at a number—we are successful about 50 percent of the time. Maybe one out of two, or two out of four, will make it.
Gardiner:	That's a pretty fair success rate compared to national ratios.
Snook:	Yes it is. Now keep in mind that when you're talking professional fire fighters, you are dealing with people who at one time were chosen as the cream of the crop. They've got a lot of mental and physical attributes to start with: They're good employees. They're at the top of their class, so to speak, academically, and as far as having the physical ability to compete in a tough workplace. They're good people. We're making good progress. Time-wise, the people who have surrounded themselves with drugs and alcohol are tough. They're sneaky, they're sly, and they know how to use the system. I would say the majority of the time spent in my human resources department, and with personnel, is spent with these types of people, because if they don't successfully make it through the program, you're in the traditional process of trying to build a case and take these people out of the organization, but based on documentation and the traditional types of discipline that most people are accustomed to. A lot of time goes into working with the system properly as far as the hearings and documentation and followups are concerned: to document the concerns and complaints and problems you have with this type of employee.
Gardiner:	This is apparently time that is tedious, Jack, but it is time that is necessary and well spent when you have

that tough choice—when you do have to terminate someone.

Snook: You have to. Yes it is, it is tough, but it is necessary because in the absence of dealing with this problem, the problem is still there. Unfortunately, it tends to affect the rest of the work group and the workplace, and so the productivity and the attitude and the morale of the people who have to work with this person tend to deteriorate. It is very quickly compounded if not dealt with properly. The price that you pay to deal with it is based on the fact that, yes, you can turn around half of these people and, yes, you are cleaning up the environment for your good employees. So the price is probably ten times returned because of the better environment you've got for the employees who don't have these types of problems.

ENDNOTES

1. Morton Grodzins, *America Betrayed: Politics and the Japanese Evacuation* (Chicago: The University of Chicago Press, 1949): 2.

2. David Sanger, "Dissenting Shuttle Engineers on Different Paths One Year Later," *The Oregonian,* January 28, 1987 (from the *New York Times News Service*).

TOUGH-MINDED MANAGEMENT
GETS THE JOB DONE

Let the Work Group Solve the Problem for You

In many organizations, both public and private, informal work groups are a powerful force in getting the job done. The sensitive manager will be quick to spot such a group: They typically work on their own in a relatively private or remote setting; they have a strong informal leader (who is usually in the same job category, or on the same organizational level as the other members of the group); they have a strong sense of belonging and pride (often they have a group nickname or logo, and they socialize a lot off the job); and they are a wonderful asset to a manager who has the common sense to leave them alone while they accomplish the job.*

If a tough-minded manager is fortunate enough to have, and to recognize, a productive informal group, the group can be a major asset in managerial problem solving. Because these groups pride themselves on a high level of performance and getting the job done without the help of management, they are also highly motivated to take effective action when a problem-employee situation develops. The leader of the group is the person to contact, of course, and all the tough-minded manager has to say is something like, "You've probably noticed, George, that Harry's been coming in late a lot lately, and I know you're prob-

---

*As Rensis Likert pointed out in his classic volume, *The Human Organization* (New York: McGraw-Hill, 1967), authoritarian or unenlightened management often deliberately breaks up such highly-productive informal groups because they sometimes ignore or circumvent formal rules and policies. Woe become the witless organization that does not heed the timeless American dictum, "If it ain't broke, don't fix it!"

Nice-Guy Lesson #9

Our hero has given up his gutless nice-guy image and becomes an effective problem solver!

ably going to be talking to him. I'll be happy to, though, if you'd rather I did it."

Such a statement is recommended because it does two important things for the tough-minded manager: (1) It recognizes the role and importance of the informal work leader, and (2) it reasserts the legitimate authority of the manager, and his or her willingness to use that authority if need be. Above all, the manager does not want to cop out in the presence of a strong work group; to abdicate is to lose their respect. Maintaining the respect of the work group is particularly important, since a work group that is loyal to management will not only be productive, it will also give management time to deal with other problems.

MORE TOUGH-MINDED MANAGEMENT GETS THE JOB DONE

From Hiring to Firing: Mistakes to Avoid

While the process of effective (but gentle) termination of a problem employee has already been dealt with in these pages, this process is so fraught with anxiety, and so often badly bungled, that some additional (and rather preachy) comments seem to be in order. Legally, the entire issue of firing has been the subject of considerable attention in the courts in recent years, and without going into all of the details and niceties of the issue, in general, there has been significant curtailment of the right of an employer to "terminate at will," i.e. to fire even a senior employee for no reason, and for the employee to have no legal remedy. Termination at will, we might note, applied only in those situations where there was no union agreement, or some other contractual relationship between employer and employee.

Increasingly, employees who are discharged abruptly and (in their minds) unfairly, sue. Increasingly, they win their cases, or handsome out-of-court settlements, when the courts find that the employer has acted in an unfair, capricious, arbitrary, prejudicial, or stupid manner. Because it may cost a large company upwards of $200,000 to defend itself in a wrongful-firing case, the following list of "don'ts" is designed to save the intelligent employer both time and money.

1. When hiring an employee, *do not* state or imply that the job is permanent, or that the employee has a contract, if this is not the case. Even a statement like, "You're likely to get a promotion in two years," may be interpreted by the courts as an implied contractual agreement.
2. If an employee has made a good-faith complaint about the organization or its manager, or has reported an unethical or illegal activity of the organization, *do not* harass the employee in any way—do not attempt to demote him, do not abuse him verbally or physically, do not shun him or move his physical work location, do not deny him any normal privileges, and (above all) *do not* attempt to fire him.
3. If the company *does not* have a progressive discipline policy, write one and implement it. Have the legal department, or a competent outside attorney, review the policy before putting it in place.
4. If the company does have a progressive discipline policy, *do not* skip any of the steps required by that policy when formal disciplinary action becomes necessary.
5. When firing an employee, if this is required, *do not* make any references to that individual's personal characteristics or problems. Do not say things like, "We're canning you because you're a drunk," or "Your personality is so obnoxious no one around here can stand you." Do not say these things even when they are true.
6. In any case involving discipline or termination, *do not* ignore the advice of the personnel or legal department. If the advice of either of these departments seems questionable or dubious, get a second opinion before taking any action.
7. Above all, in disciplining or firing *any* employee, *never* make any reference to that person's race, sex, nationality, appearance, color, religion, emotional health, physical health, or personal worth. Even if you are a bigot, and are so unfortunate as to think bigoted thoughts, keep your thoughts to yourself.

INDEX

ABOUT THE AUTHOR

Gareth S. Gardiner has a Ph.D. in psychology from Princeton University. He has been a consultant to government and industry, specializing in the effective management of problem employees and ethical problems faced by managers.

His business experience includes founding a restaurant in St. Louis, establishing a direct-mail business, and running a construction company to rehabilitate historic buildings. He is the founder and president of the Smith Collins Company.